NORWAY : A TRAVEL GUIDE

ZION HALLEL

All rights reserved. No part of this publication may be reproduced, distributed, or transmitted in any form or by any means, including photocopying, recording, or other electronic or mechanical methods, without the prior written permission of the publisher, except in the case of brief quotations embodied in critical reviews and certain other noncommercial uses permitted by copyright law.

Copyright © (ZION HALLEL) (2023).

TABLE OF CONTENTS

Introduction to Norway — 7
Chapter 1. — 11
   Geography and Climate — 11
   History and Culture — 13
   Norway Today — 16
Chapter 2. Planning Your Trip — 21
   When to Visit — 21
   Entry Requirements and Visa Information — 23
   Transportation in Norway — 27
   Currency and Money Matters — 30
   Language and Communication — 33
Chapter 3. Exploring Oslo — 37
   Overview of Oslo — 37
   Top Attractions — 39
   Museums and Galleries — 42
   Parks and Outdoor Activities — 45
   Shopping and Dining — 48
Chapter 4. The Fjords of Western Norway — 53
   Bergen and the Gateway to the Fjords — 53
   Geirangerfjord — 55
   Sognefjord — 58
   Hardangerfjord — 60
   Activities and Hiking Routes — 63
Chapter 5. Northern Norway and the Arctic — 67
   Tromsø and the Midnight Sun — 67
   Lofoten Islands — 69
   North Cape — 73

  Sami Culture and Reindeer Sledding   76
  Northern Lights Viewing   78

Chapter 6. Coastal Gems and Islands   **83**
  Ålesund and Art Nouveau Architecture   83
  Trondheim and Nidaros Cathedral   85
  The Atlantic Road   87
  Røros Mining Town   89
  Islands of Southern Norway   92

Chapter 7. Outdoor Adventures   **95**
  Hiking and Trekking Routes   95
  Wildlife Safaris   97
  Skiing and Winter Sports   99
  Fishing and Sailing   103
  Camping and National Parks   105

Chapter 8. Norwegian Cuisine and Local Delicacies   **109**
  Traditional Norwegian Dishes   109
  Seafood and Fish Specialties   111
  Scandinavian Desserts and Pastries   114
  Culinary Festivals and Food Markets   117
  Recommended Restaurants and Cafes   119

Chapter 9. Practical Information and Travel Tips 123
  Accommodation Options   123
  Health and Safety   126
  Etiquette and Customs   129
  Useful Phrases and Basic Norwegian   132
  Packing List and Essential Gear   133

Introduction to Norway

Welcome to the land of majestic fjords, breathtaking landscapes, and vibrant Nordic culture Norway! Nestled in the heart of Scandinavia, Norway is a captivating destination that offers a remarkable blend of natural wonders and urban sophistication. From the ethereal beauty of the Northern Lights dancing across the sky to the bustling streets of Oslo, Norway never fails to enchant its visitors.

Renowned for its stunning fjords, Norway boasts a coastline adorned with deep, narrow inlets flanked by towering cliffs, creating a surreal panorama that leaves travelers awe-struck. Whether you embark on a scenic cruise through the iconic Geirangerfjord, explore the lesser-known gems of Sognefjord, or hike along the picturesque Nærøyfjord, you'll find yourself immersed in a world of sheer tranquility and awe-inspiring grandeur.

Beyond its natural splendor, Norway's cities are vibrant hubs of culture and innovation. Oslo, the cosmopolitan capital, pulsates with energy, blending modern architecture with historic landmarks such as the iconic Akershus Fortress and the Royal Palace. Museums like the Viking Ship

Museum and the Munch Museum showcase Norway's rich history and artistic heritage, while the trendy neighbourhoods of Grünerløkka and Aker Brygge offer a plethora of stylish boutiques, hip cafes, and buzzing nightlife.

For adventure enthusiasts, Norway presents a playground of thrilling activities. Embark on a thrilling dog-sledding expedition through the Arctic wilderness, challenge yourself with a hike to Trolltunga—a jutting rock formation high above a deep fjord—or experience the exhilaration of skiing in the winter wonderland of Trysil or Hemsedal. Nature lovers will also find delight in exploring Norway's national parks, where they can witness diverse flora and fauna, go wildlife spotting, and indulge in hiking, biking, and kayaking amidst awe-inspiring landscapes.

Norway's cultural tapestry is woven with the spirit of exploration and discovery. The country's seafaring history is brought to life in cities like Bergen, where the UNESCO-listed Bryggen Wharf is a testament to the Hanseatic League's maritime legacy. The Sami indigenous culture in the northern regions offers a glimpse into a way of life shaped by a deep connection with nature and reindeer herding traditions.

With a reputation for sustainable living, Norway sets a remarkable example for environmental conservation and eco-tourism. Its commitment to preserving its natural wonders can be seen in initiatives like the world's first all-electric car ferry and the sustainable architecture of the Arctic Cathedral in Tromsø. Travelers to Norway have the opportunity to engage in responsible travel practices, embrace eco-friendly accommodations, and support local communities that prioritize the well-being of the planet.

So whether you seek the serenity of untamed wilderness, the excitement of outdoor adventures, or the charm of culturally rich cities, Norway invites you to embark on a journey that will captivate your senses and leave an indelible mark on your soul. Get ready to be enchanted by the land of the midnight sun, the land of the Vikings, welcome to Norway!

Chapter 1.

Geography and Climate

Norway, located in Northern Europe, is renowned for its breathtaking natural beauty, encompassing a diverse range of landscapes, fjords, and scenic vistas. The country's geography and climate play a significant role in shaping its stunning environment and making it an attractive destination for travellers.

Geographically, Norway is characterised by its rugged coastline, towering mountains, deep valleys, and pristine lakes. The country shares borders with Sweden, Finland, and Russia, while its coastline stretches for over 25,000 kilometres, including numerous fjords, islands, and archipelagos. Some of the notable fjords, such as the UNESCO-listed Geirangerfjord and Nærøyfjord, offer awe-inspiring views of cascading waterfalls, steep cliffs, and emerald green waters. The fjords are not only a visual delight but also provide ample opportunities for activities like kayaking, boating, and wildlife spotting.

Norway's climate is influenced by its high latitude and the warm Gulf Stream, resulting in diverse weather patterns across the country. Generally,

Norway experiences cool summers and relatively mild winters. However, due to its varied topography, weather conditions can vary significantly from region to region. The coastal areas benefit from the tempering effect of the Gulf Stream, resulting in milder temperatures and more precipitation, while the inland regions and higher altitudes experience colder winters with heavier snowfall.

The western coastal areas, including Bergen and Stavanger, have a maritime climate characterized by mild winters, cool summers, and high precipitation throughout the year. The Atlantic Ocean influences the climate in these regions, bringing frequent rain showers and creating lush green landscapes. The southwestern coast is particularly known for its mild climate and is often referred to as the "Norwegian Riviera."

Moving inland, towards the central and northern parts of Norway, the climate becomes more continental. Cities like Oslo and Trondheim experience colder winters with temperatures often dropping below freezing, while summers can be pleasantly warm. In the northernmost regions, such as Tromsø and Kirkenes, the climate is subarctic, with long, cold winters and shorter, relatively mild summers. The famous phenomenon of the midnight sun can be observed in the northernmost parts of Norway during summer, where the sun remains visible 24 hours a day.

Norway's varied geography and climate offer a plethora of outdoor activities and scenic landscapes for travelers to explore. From hiking and skiing in the mountains to cruising through majestic fjords, Norway's natural wonders are sure to captivate any visitor. Whether you're seeking an adventure-filled vacation or simply wish to immerse yourself in the tranquility of nature, Norway's geography and climate provide an ideal setting for an unforgettable travel experience.

History and Culture

Norway boasts a rich history and vibrant culture, deeply rooted in its ancient Norse heritage and shaped by its evolution through the centuries. Exploring the history and immersing oneself in the unique cultural traditions of Norway can be a fascinating and rewarding experience for travellers.

Historically, Norway was inhabited by various tribes and clans before the unification of the country under the rule of King Harald Fairhair in the 9th century. During the Viking Age, which spanned from the 8th to the 11th century, Norwegian seafarers and explorers embarked on daring expeditions, leaving their mark on European history. The Vikings were renowned for their shipbuilding skills, seafaring prowess, and trading networks that extended across the continent. Today, visitors can delve into Norway's Viking legacy through the numerous museums, archaeological sites, and historical reenactments that showcase their fascinating culture and seafaring achievements.

One of the most significant events in Norwegian history is the signing of the Kalmar Union in 1397, which united Norway, Sweden, and Denmark under a single monarch. The union lasted for several centuries, during which Norway faced periods of political and economic challenges, including the loss of its autonomy. However, the early 19th century marked the resurgence of Norwegian nationalism, leading to the dissolution of the union in 1905 and the establishment of an independent Norwegian monarchy.

Norway's culture is deeply intertwined with its stunning natural surroundings. The country's breathtaking landscapes, encompassing fjords, mountains, and forests, have inspired its art, literature, and folklore for centuries. The works of famous Norwegian painters like Edvard Munch and Johan Christian Dahl reflect the country's unique light, dramatic landscapes, and deep connection to nature. Visitors can explore the vibrant art scene in cities like Oslo and Bergen, where world-class museums and galleries showcase both contemporary and traditional Norwegian art.

Norwegian folklore and mythology are an integral part of the country's cultural fabric. Tales of trolls, giants, and mythical creatures have been passed down through generations, adding an enchanting element to Norway's cultural identity. Traditional Norwegian music, such as the haunting melodies of the Hardanger fiddle, captures the essence of Norwegian folk traditions and can be experienced through live performances and folk festivals.

Cuisine is another aspect of Norwegian culture that should not be missed. With its proximity to the sea and abundance of natural resources, Norway offers a variety of seafood dishes, including salmon, cod, and herring, prepared in traditional and modern ways. Traditional Norwegian cuisine also includes dishes like lutefisk (dried fish), rakfisk (fermented fish), and reindeer meat, providing visitors with a unique gastronomic experience.

Furthermore, Norwegians value their outdoor lifestyle and have a strong connection to nature. The concept of "friluftsliv," meaning "open-air living," emphasises spending time outdoors, whether it's hiking, skiing, or simply enjoying the tranquillity of the forests and fjords. This cultural appreciation for nature is reflected in Norway's emphasis on sustainable practices, conservation efforts, and eco-friendly tourism.

Exploring the history and immersing oneself in the culture of Norway offers a fascinating journey through time and a deeper understanding of the country's unique identity. From the legacy of the Vikings to the enchanting folklore, from world-class art to delicious cuisine, Norway's history and culture add depth and richness to any travel experience.

Norway Today

Today, Norway stands as a captivating blend of traditional charm and contemporary sophistication, making it an ideal destination for travellers seeking diverse experiences. Let's explore what makes Norway an extraordinary place to visit today.

Natural Beauty:

Norway's natural beauty is unparalleled, boasting majestic fjords, towering mountains, picturesque valleys, and enchanting forests. One of the most iconic attractions is the breathtaking Geirangerfjord, a UNESCO World Heritage site known for its pristine waters, cascading waterfalls, and dramatic cliffs. Visitors can also explore the famous Trolltunga, a striking rock formation that offers awe-inspiring panoramic views.

Urban Delights:
Norway's cities are equally captivating, combining modernity with a deep appreciation for nature. Oslo, the capital city, offers a vibrant urban experience with its cutting-edge architecture, world-class museums, and a thriving culinary scene. The iconic Opera House and Vigeland Park are must-visit attractions that showcase the city's commitment to art and design.

Cultural Heritage:
Norway's rich cultural heritage is visible in its preserved medieval towns, Viking history, and Sami indigenous culture. In Bergen, the charming UNESCO-listed Bryggen Wharf takes you back in time with its colorful wooden buildings. Trondheim, another historic city, offers the

incredible Nidaros Cathedral, a pilgrimage site and a masterpiece of Gothic architecture.

Outdoor Adventures:
Norway's rugged terrain provides countless opportunities for outdoor enthusiasts. From hiking and skiing in the mountains to kayaking and fishing in the fjords, Norway is a playground for adventure seekers. In winter, the country transforms into a wonderland for winter sports, with world-class ski resorts like Trysil and Hemsedal attracting enthusiasts from around the globe.

Sustainable Practices:
Norway is at the forefront of sustainability and environmental consciousness. The country has embraced renewable energy sources and encourages eco-friendly practices. Visitors can experience this commitment firsthand through eco-lodges, sustainable transportation options, and the opportunity to participate in eco-conscious activities such as glacier walks and wildlife safaris that promote conservation and respect for nature.

Northern Lights:
No guide to Norway would be complete without mentioning the mesmerising Northern Lights, also known as the Aurora Borealis. The Arctic regions of

Norway, including Tromsø and the Lofoten Islands, offer some of the best chances to witness this celestial phenomenon. Imagine standing under a dancing sky, bathed in shades of green, pink, and purple – an unforgettable experience that is best observed during the winter months.

Norway today captures the essence of a progressive and nature-loving nation, where modernity intertwines harmoniously with its awe-inspiring landscapes and cultural heritage. Whether you're seeking outdoor adventures, cultural exploration, or simply a place to reconnect with nature, Norway has something to offer every traveler. Immerse yourself in its beauty, embrace its sustainability ethos, and create lifelong memories in this Nordic wonderland.

Chapter 2. Planning Your Trip

When to Visit

Norway, with its breathtaking landscapes, majestic fjords, and vibrant cities, is a country that captivates visitors all year round. However, the best time to visit Norway depends on the type of experience you're seeking and the activities you wish to engage in. Whether you're drawn to the dazzling Northern Lights, planning a summer hiking adventure, or seeking a winter wonderland, Norway has something to offer in every season.

Summer (June to August):
The summer months are the most popular time to visit Norway, especially for outdoor enthusiasts. The weather is mild, with temperatures ranging from 15 to 25 degrees Celsius (59 to 77 degrees Fahrenheit) in most areas. The long days allow for ample daylight, giving you plenty of time to explore the stunning landscapes, hike in the national parks, or cruise along the fjords. The famous midnight sun is also a highlight during this time, particularly in the northern regions. It's an ideal season for outdoor activities, festivals, and experiencing the vibrant cultural scene in cities like Oslo and Bergen.

Autumn (September to November):

Autumn in Norway is a season of vibrant colors as the foliage changes to hues of red, orange, and gold. The weather starts to cool down, and the crowds thin out compared to the peak summer season. It's a great time to explore the picturesque countryside, go hiking in the mountains, or take a scenic road trip along the coastal routes. September and October are also excellent months for witnessing the magical Northern Lights in the northern parts of the country. Be prepared for varying weather conditions and pack layers to stay comfortable.

Winter (December to February):
Norway transforms into a true winter wonderland during the colder months. The snow-covered landscapes create a magical atmosphere, and winter sports enthusiasts flock to the country for activities like skiing, snowboarding, and dog sledding. The northern regions, such as Tromsø and Alta, offer excellent opportunities to witness the mesmerizing Northern Lights. Winter temperatures can be quite cold, ranging from -10 to 5 degrees Celsius (14 to 41 degrees Fahrenheit), so make sure to dress warmly and be aware of shorter daylight hours.

Spring (March to May):
As the snow begins to melt, spring emerges in Norway, bringing with it the promise of renewal

and blooming nature. March and April are still considered winter months in many parts of the country, but by May, the temperatures start to rise, and nature awakens. Spring is an excellent time to visit if you prefer milder weather and fewer tourists. It's a great time to explore the cities, witness the stunning waterfalls as the snow melts, and embark on coastal cruises to see the diverse wildlife, including whales and seals.

Ultimately, the best time to visit Norway depends on your personal preferences and the experiences you're seeking. Each season has its own unique charm, and whether you're chasing the Northern Lights, eager to hike amidst picturesque landscapes, or simply want to explore the rich cultural heritage, Norway is a destination that promises unforgettable experiences throughout the year.

Entry Requirements and Visa Information

Travelling to Norway offers an opportunity to immerse yourself in the country's stunning natural beauty, vibrant cities, and rich cultural heritage. Before planning your trip, it's essential to understand the entry requirements and visa information for Norway. Here's a guide to help you navigate the process smoothly.

Visa Requirements:
Norway is a member of the Schengen Agreement, which means that citizens of many countries do not need a visa for short-term visits of up to 90 days within a 180-day period. If you are a citizen of one of the Schengen Agreement member countries, such as the United States, Canada, Australia, New Zealand, or most European countries, you can enter Norway as a tourist or for business purposes without a visa. However, it's crucial to check the specific visa requirements based on your nationality and the purpose of your visit to ensure compliance with the latest regulations.

Passport Validity:
To enter Norway, you must have a valid passport that remains valid for at least three months beyond your planned departure date. It's advisable to renew your passport if it has less than six months of validity to avoid any issues during your trip.

Visa-Free Entry:
If you are a citizen of a country that has a visa waiver agreement with the Schengen area, you can travel to Norway without a visa. This includes countries such as the United States, Canada, Australia, New Zealand, Japan, South Korea, and

many others. However, it's important to note that the purpose of your visit must be for tourism, business meetings, attending conferences, or visiting friends and relatives. If you plan to work, study, or stay in Norway for a longer period, you will need to obtain the appropriate visa or residence permit before your arrival.

Length of Stay:
As a tourist or business traveler, you can stay in Norway and the Schengen Area for up to 90 days within a 180-day period. The 180-day period is calculated backward from the date of your entry into any Schengen country. It's important to keep track of your duration of stay and plan your itinerary accordingly to ensure compliance with the visa regulations.

Additional Requirements:
While no visa is required for short-term visits, immigration authorities may request the following documentation upon arrival:

1. Proof of accommodation: Provide details of your accommodation, such as hotel reservations or an invitation letter from your host if you are staying with friends or relatives.

2. Sufficient funds: Carry enough funds to cover your expenses during your stay in Norway, such as cash, credit cards, or traveler's checks. While there is no specific amount stated, it's recommended to have enough to support yourself without relying on public assistance.

3. Return ticket: Show proof of a return or onward ticket to your home country or a destination outside the Schengen Area.

4. Travel insurance: It is highly recommended to have travel insurance that covers medical expenses and emergency repatriation. Although not mandatory, it can provide peace of mind during your trip.

It's crucial to note that visa regulations and entry requirements can change, so it's advisable to consult the official website of the Norwegian Directorate of Immigration or contact the Norwegian embassy or consulate in your home country for the most up-to-date and accurate information.

By understanding the entry requirements and visa information for Norway, you can plan your trip confidently and ensure a smooth and hassle-free travel experience to this captivating Scandinavian destination.

Transportation in Norway

Norway, known for its stunning natural beauty and picturesque landscapes, offers an efficient and well-connected transportation system that allows travellers to explore the country with ease. Whether you prefer to journey by land, air, or sea, Norway has various options to suit your needs. Here is a guide to transportation in Norway to help you navigate this enchanting Scandinavian country.

1. Air Travel:
Norway boasts several well-connected airports, making it convenient for international travelers to reach different regions of the country. Oslo Airport Gardermoen is the largest and busiest airport, serving as a major hub for both domestic and international flights. Other notable airports include Bergen Airport Flesland, Stavanger Airport Sola, and Trondheim Airport Værnes. From these airports, you can easily reach various cities and towns in Norway through domestic flights or connect to other international destinations.

2. Trains:

Norway's railway network is extensive and offers a comfortable and scenic way to explore the country. The Norwegian State Railways, known as Vy, operates regular train services connecting major cities such as Oslo, Bergen, Trondheim, and Stavanger. The trains are renowned for their punctuality, comfort, and breathtaking views of the Norwegian countryside. The famous Flåm Railway, considered one of the most picturesque train journeys in the world, takes you through dramatic fjords and mountainous landscapes.

3. Buses:
Buses are a popular mode of transportation for both short and long distances in Norway. The extensive bus network covers even the most remote regions of the country, ensuring that you can reach various destinations. Nettbuss and NOR-WAY Bussekspress are two major bus companies that provide regular services between cities, towns, and rural areas. Buses are comfortable, equipped with modern amenities, and offer scenic views during your journey.

4. Car Rental:
Renting a car in Norway is a fantastic option for travellers who want to explore at their own pace and venture off the beaten path. The country has

well-maintained roads and highways, making road trips a popular choice. Several international and local car rental companies operate throughout Norway, with rental offices available at major airports and cities. It's important to note that driving in Norway may involve toll roads and ferries, so it's advisable to familiarize yourself with the regulations and plan your routes accordingly.

5. Ferries:
Given its long coastline and numerous fjords, ferries are an integral part of Norway's transportation system. They provide a unique and scenic way to travel between different regions, especially in the western and northern parts of the country. Popular ferry routes include those connecting the mainland to the enchanting Norwegian fjords, such as the Geirangerfjord, Sognefjord, and Hardangerfjord. Ferry services also operate to connect Norway with neighboring countries like Denmark and Sweden.

6. Public Transportation:
Norway's cities have excellent public transportation systems, making it convenient to explore urban areas. Oslo, in particular, has an efficient network of buses, trams, and the Oslo Metro (T-bane). Trondheim, Bergen, Stavanger, and other major

cities also offer reliable public transportation options. Purchasing an electronic travel card or individual tickets is easy, and these can be used interchangeably on buses, trams, and trains within a specific region.

Overall, Norway offers a diverse range of transportation options that cater to different travel preferences. Whether you prefer the convenience of flying, the scenic beauty of train journeys, the flexibility of road trips, or the serenity of ferry rides, you can explore Norway's breathtaking landscapes and charming cities with ease. Plan your itinerary wisely and enjoy your unforgettable journey through this captivating Nordic country.

Currency and Money Matters

When planning a trip to Norway, it's essential to familiarise yourself with the country's currency and money matters to ensure a smooth and hassle-free experience. Here's a guide to help you navigate the world of currency in Norway:

Currency:
The official currency of Norway is the Norwegian Krone (NOK). The krone is abbreviated as "kr" and is further divided into 100 øre. Banknotes come in denominations of 50 kr, 100 kr, 200 kr, 500 kr, and

1,000 kr, while coins are available in denominations of 1 kr, 5 kr, 10 kr, and 20 kr.

Currency Exchange:
It's advisable to exchange your currency for Norwegian Krone before your trip or upon arrival in Norway. Currency exchange services can be found at international airports, major train stations, and in city centers. Banks and specialized exchange offices ("Forex" or "Currency Exchange") offer competitive rates. It's recommended to compare rates and fees to get the best deal.

Credit Cards and Debit Cards:
Credit and debit cards are widely accepted in Norway, and most establishments, including hotels, restaurants, shops, and attractions, will readily accept cards for payment. International credit cards such as Visa and Mastercard are commonly used. However, it's always a good idea to carry some cash for smaller establishments or places that might not accept cards.

ATMs:
ATMs, known as "Minibank" in Norwegian, are easily accessible throughout Norway. They can be found at banks, shopping centers, and transportation hubs. ATMs accept most major

international debit and credit cards, allowing you to withdraw cash in Norwegian Krone. Keep in mind that some ATMs may charge a fee for withdrawals, so it's advisable to check with your bank beforehand.

Tipping:
Tipping in Norway is not as common or expected as it is in some other countries. However, if you receive exceptional service, it's appreciated to leave a small tip. In restaurants, a service charge is often included in the bill, but it's customary to round up the amount or leave a small additional tip. Taxi drivers also appreciate a small tip for good service.

Prices and Cost of Living:
Norway is known for being one of the more expensive countries to visit. Prices for accommodation, dining, transportation, and goods can be higher compared to many other destinations. However, the quality of services and products generally matches the higher price tag. It's important to budget accordingly and be prepared for the higher cost of living while enjoying the unique experiences Norway has to offer.

Value Added Tax (VAT) Refund:

Visitors from outside the European Union (EU) can claim a refund on the Value Added Tax (VAT) paid on eligible goods purchased in Norway. To be eligible, make sure to ask for a VAT refund form (Tax-Free Shopping form) when making your purchases and follow the necessary procedures for obtaining the refund at the airport before departing Norway.

It's always a good idea to inform your bank or credit card company about your travel plans to avoid any issues with card usage abroad. With a good understanding of Norway's currency and money matters, you can focus on enjoying your trip without any financial concerns.

Language and Communication

When travelling to Norway, understanding the language and having effective communication can greatly enhance your experience and interactions with locals. Here's a guide to help you navigate language and communication in Norway:

Official Language:
The official language of Norway is Norwegian. There are two forms of written Norwegian: Bokmål (literally "book language") and Nynorsk (literally "new Norwegian"). Bokmål is more widely used and

is the main written language in most urban areas, while Nynorsk is more prevalent in certain rural regions. However, English is widely spoken and understood throughout the country, particularly among younger generations and in tourist areas.

English Proficiency:
Norwegians are generally proficient in English, with many locals speaking it fluently. In fact, Norway consistently ranks among the top non-native English-speaking countries in the world. You can comfortably communicate in English with most Norwegians, especially in urban areas, hotels, restaurants, and tourist attractions. However, it's always polite to learn a few basic Norwegian phrases to show your interest and respect for the local culture.

Basic Norwegian Phrases:
Learning a few basic Norwegian phrases can go a long way in making connections and showing appreciation for the local language. Here are a few useful phrases:

- Hello: Hei (pronounced "hay")
- Goodbye: Ha det (pronounced "hah deh")
- Please: Vær så snill (pronounced "vair saw snill")
- Thank you: Takk (pronounced "tahk")

- Yes: Ja (pronounced "yah")
- No: Nei (pronounced "nay")
- Excuse me: Unnskyld (pronounced "oonskild")
- Do you speak English?: Snakker du engelsk? (pronounced "snahker doo ENG-elsk?")
- I don't understand: Jeg forstår ikke (pronounced "yay for-stohr eet-eh")

Translation Tools:
If you want to delve deeper into the Norwegian language or find yourself in a situation where communication is challenging, translation tools can be handy. Online translation websites, mobile apps, or phrasebooks can help you bridge the language gap and assist with understanding signs, menus, or written information in Norwegian.

Signage and Information:
In most tourist areas, signs, menus, and information boards are often displayed in both Norwegian and English. Museums, attractions, and transportation systems also provide information in English, making it easier for international travelers to navigate and understand. If you find yourself in more remote areas or smaller towns, English signage might be less common, but locals are usually helpful in assisting visitors.

Cultural Etiquette:
Norwegians appreciate visitors who make an effort to learn about their culture and language. While English is widely spoken, using a few Norwegian phrases, such as greetings and simple pleasantries, can help establish a friendly rapport. Norwegians are generally polite and reserved, so being respectful and maintaining a calm demeanor during interactions is appreciated.

With English widely spoken and understood, language barriers are minimal when traveling in Norway. However, embracing the local language and culture by learning a few basic Norwegian phrases can enrich your experience and show your appreciation for this captivating Scandinavian country.

Chapter 3. Exploring Oslo

Overview of Oslo

Oslo, the capital city of Norway, is a vibrant and cosmopolitan destination that offers a perfect blend of natural beauty, cultural attractions, and a high-quality urban lifestyle. Situated on the southern coast of the country, Oslo is nestled between the Oslofjord and the lush forests of Nordmarka, creating a stunning backdrop for the city's scenic landscapes.

One of the distinguishing features of Oslo is its commitment to sustainability and environmental preservation. It has been awarded the title of European Green Capital in recognition of its efforts to promote eco-friendly practices and develop a sustainable urban environment. This dedication is evident in the city's extensive public transportation system, which includes trams, buses, and ferries, making it easy for visitors to explore and navigate the city.

The city centre of Oslo is compact and walkable, allowing visitors to experience its rich history, modern architecture, and lively atmosphere. The Royal Palace, situated at the end of the bustling main street, Karl Johans gate, is a prominent landmark that should not be missed. Strolling along this street will lead you to numerous shops, restaurants, and cafés, as well as important cultural institutions like the National Theater and the Oslo Cathedral.

Art and culture play a significant role in Oslo's identity, with a wealth of museums and galleries that showcase both traditional and contemporary Norwegian art. The iconic Vigeland Sculpture Park, located in the Frogner Park, is a must-visit destination, featuring over 200 sculptures created by Gustav Vigeland. The Munch Museum, dedicated to the works of renowned painter Edvard Munch, is another highlight for art enthusiasts.

For those seeking outdoor adventures, Oslo offers ample opportunities to connect with nature. The city is surrounded by forests and hills, providing excellent hiking and skiing opportunities, depending on the season. The nearby Oslofjord is also a popular spot for boating, swimming, and relaxing on the beaches during the summer months.

Food lovers will delight in Oslo's thriving culinary scene, with a wide range of restaurants and cafés offering both traditional Norwegian dishes and international cuisine. From fresh seafood to Nordic-inspired delicacies, there is something to suit every palate. Additionally, the city is known for its coffee culture, and you'll find numerous cozy cafés where you can relax and enjoy a cup of java.

Oslo's vibrant nightlife caters to various tastes, with trendy bars, clubs, and live music venues scattered throughout the city. The Grünerløkka neighbourhood, with its bohemian vibe, is particularly popular among locals and visitors alike.

In summary, Oslo offers a delightful mix of natural beauty, cultural richness, and sustainable living. Whether you're interested in exploring museums, immersing yourself in nature, or indulging in culinary delights, this Norwegian capital has something to offer every traveller.

Top Attractions

Norway, with its stunning natural landscapes and vibrant cities, offers a wealth of attractions for travellers to explore. From majestic fjords and snow-capped mountains to charming coastal towns and rich cultural heritage, Norway has something to captivate every visitor. Here are some of the top attractions in Norway that should be on your travel itinerary:

1. Geirangerfjord: Considered one of the most beautiful fjords in the world, Geirangerfjord is a UNESCO World Heritage site. Its deep blue waters, cascading waterfalls, and towering cliffs create a breathtaking panorama. Take a boat tour or hike to the viewpoints to fully appreciate its awe-inspiring beauty.

2. Bergen: Known as the "Gateway to the Fjords," Bergen is a charming coastal city with a rich history and vibrant culture. Explore the colourful wooden houses of Bryggen, a UNESCO-listed site, visit the Hanseatic Museum, and take the Fløibanen funicular for panoramic views of the city and surrounding mountains.

3. Tromsø: Located in the Arctic Circle, Tromsø is a fascinating city known for its Northern Lights and stunning natural landscapes. Visit the Arctic Cathedral, take a cable car ride to Mount Storsteinen for panoramic views, or go dog sledding or reindeer sledding for a unique Arctic experience.

4. Oslo: The capital city of Norway, Oslo offers a blend of modern architecture, cultural attractions, and outdoor activities. Visit the iconic Opera House, explore the fascinating exhibits at the

Viking Ship Museum and the Munch Museum, and stroll through the beautiful Vigeland Sculpture Park.

5. Lofoten Islands: Located above the Arctic Circle, the Lofoten Islands are renowned for their dramatic mountains, picturesque fishing villages, and pristine beaches. Explore the traditional fishing villages of Reine and Å, hike to the stunning peaks like Reinebringen, and experience the unique Midnight Sun phenomenon during the summer months.

6. Preikestolen (Pulpit Rock): Situated near Stavanger, Preikestolen is a majestic cliff rising 604 meters above the Lysefjord. Hike to the top for incredible views of the fjord and surrounding mountains. It's a popular spot for adventure seekers and nature enthusiasts.

7. Sognefjord: Known as the "King of the Fjords," Sognefjord is the longest and deepest fjord in Norway. Cruise along its serene waters, passing by picturesque villages, waterfalls, and lush valleys. Don't miss the charming village of Flam and the Flåm Railway, one of the most scenic train journeys in the world.

8. Trondheim: With its mediaeval architecture, colourful wharves, and vibrant arts scene, Trondheim is a city that seamlessly blends history and modernity. Visit the iconic Nidaros Cathedral, explore the vibrant Bakklandet district, and take a relaxing boat trip along the Nidelva River.

These are just a few of the top attractions in Norway, offering a glimpse into the country's stunning natural beauty and rich cultural heritage. Whether you're seeking adventure, tranquillity, or cultural immersion, Norway is sure to leave a lasting impression on every traveller.

Museums and Galleries

Norway is a country known for its stunning natural landscapes, rich history, and vibrant cultural scene. In addition to its breathtaking fjords, mountains, and Northern Lights, Norway is also home to a diverse range of museums and galleries that offer unique insights into the country's art, history, and culture. Whether you're an art enthusiast, history buff, or simply curious about Norway's heritage, exploring the museums and galleries in Norway is an essential part of any traveller's itinerary.

One of the must-visit museums in Norway is the Norwegian Museum of Cultural History, located in

Oslo. This open-air museum showcases the country's cultural heritage through a vast collection of historic buildings from different regions and eras. As you stroll through the museum's picturesque grounds, you'll encounter traditional Norwegian houses, farmsteads, and Sami structures. This immersive experience provides a glimpse into Norway's past and the daily lives of its inhabitants throughout history.

If you're interested in contemporary art, a visit to the Astrup Fearnley Museum in Oslo is highly recommended. This modern art museum showcases an impressive collection of international contemporary art, including works by renowned artists like Jeff Koons, Damien Hirst, and Cindy Sherman. The museum's sleek architecture and waterfront location add to the overall experience, making it a favourite among art enthusiasts.

Another significant cultural institution in Oslo is the National Gallery, which houses Norway's largest public collection of paintings, sculptures, and other art forms. The gallery's collection spans several centuries and includes works by Norwegian masters like Edvard Munch, as well as international artists such as Vincent van Gogh and Pablo Picasso. The iconic painting "The Scream" by Edvard Munch is undoubtedly the gallery's most famous and recognizable piece.

For those interested in maritime history, the Viking Ship Museum in Oslo offers a captivating journey into the Viking Age. Here, you can marvel at remarkably preserved Viking longships, including the Oseberg ship, Gokstad ship, and Tune ship. These ancient vessels are beautifully displayed, providing insights into the seafaring and cultural traditions of the Vikings. The museum also features an array of artefacts recovered from Viking burial sites, offering a glimpse into their daily lives and customs.

Moving beyond Oslo, the Bergen Maritime Museum in Bergen is a captivating destination for maritime enthusiasts. Located on the historic Bryggen wharf, the museum highlights Bergen's role as a significant port city throughout history. The exhibits cover various aspects of seafaring, including shipbuilding, fishing, and trade. The museum's interactive displays and multimedia presentations make it an engaging experience for visitors of all ages.

If you find yourself in Trondheim, a visit to the Nidaros Cathedral and Archbishop's Palace Museum is a must. The cathedral, dating back to the 11th century, is one of Norway's most important religious and historical landmarks. Inside the museum, you can explore the cathedral's rich history, royal regalia, and mediaeval artefacts. Climbing the tower rewards visitors with panoramic views of the city and surrounding landscapes.

These are just a few examples of the many museums and galleries that Norway has to offer. From art and history to maritime heritage and cultural traditions, each institution provides a unique and enriching experience. Whether you're a history enthusiast, art lover, or simply curious traveler, Norway's museums and galleries are sure to leave a lasting impression and deepen your understanding of this beautiful country.

Parks and Outdoor Activities

Welcome to Norway, a country known for its breathtaking natural beauty and abundance of outdoor activities. Whether you're a nature enthusiast, an adventure seeker, or simply looking to unwind amidst stunning landscapes, Norway offers a wide range of parks and outdoor experiences that will leave you in awe. Here are some highlights to include in your Norwegian adventure:

1. Norway's National Parks:
Norway boasts numerous national parks, each offering its own unique charm. Jotunheimen National Park, situated in the heart of the country, is home to Norway's highest peaks, including Galdhøpiggen. Hardangervidda National Park, the largest in Norway, showcases vast plateaus, majestic waterfalls, and incredible hiking trails. For coastal beauty, explore the picturesque landscapes of Lofoten Islands or the dramatic fjords of Jostedalsbreen National Park, where you can witness glaciers up close.

2. Hiking and Trekking:
Norway is a paradise for hikers and trekkers, with an extensive network of well-marked trails catering to all levels of expertise. The iconic Trolltunga, a spectacular rock formation jutting out above a deep fjord, is a must-visit for adventurers seeking a thrilling experience. Other popular trails include the Pulpit Rock (Preikestolen) near Stavanger and the Romsdalseggen Ridge in Åndalsnes. Remember to pack appropriate gear and check weather conditions before embarking on your hike.

3. Fjord Cruises and Kayaking:
Norway's fjords are among the country's most mesmerising natural wonders. Take a leisurely fjord

cruise to soak in the awe-inspiring beauty of UNESCO-listed sites like Geirangerfjord or Nærøyfjord. For a more immersive experience, try kayaking through the fjords, allowing you to explore hidden coves, encounter wildlife, and feel a deep connection to nature.

4. Northern Lights Viewing:
If you visit Norway during the winter months, witnessing the enchanting Northern Lights (Aurora Borealis) is an absolute must. Head to remote regions such as Tromsø or the Lofoten Islands for the best chances of catching this celestial spectacle. Many tour operators offer guided Northern Lights excursions, complete with cozy winter cabins and knowledgeable guides to enhance your experience.

5. Wildlife and Bird Watching:
Norway's diverse ecosystems are home to a wide range of wildlife. Experience encounters with reindeer, moose, and arctic foxes in their natural habitats. Along the coast, spot seals, whales, and seabirds like puffins. Svalbard, an archipelago in the Arctic, is an excellent destination for spotting polar bears, walruses, and migratory birds.

6. Cycling and Skiing:

Norway's vast landscapes are ideal for cycling enthusiasts. Pedal along scenic routes like the Rallarvegen, a historic mountain road, or explore the serene trails around the Hardangerfjord. During winter, Norway transforms into a winter wonderland, offering world-class skiing and snowboarding opportunities. Hit the slopes in popular destinations like Trysil, Hemsedal, or Lillehammer.

Remember to respect the environment and follow Norway's outdoor etiquette. Plan your activities well in advance, especially during peak tourist seasons. Embrace the Norwegian concept of "friluftsliv," which translates to "outdoor life," and immerse yourself in the stunning natural wonders that Norway has to offer.

Shopping and Dining

When it comes to shopping and dining, Norway offers a unique blend of modern trends and traditional Nordic charm. From bustling city centres to quaint coastal towns, the country provides an array of options for visitors seeking retail therapy and culinary delights.Here, we will explore the vibrant shopping scene and mouth watering dining experiences that await you in Norway.

Shopping in Norway:

1. Oslo: As Norway's capital and largest city, Oslo is a shopaholic's paradise. The pedestrian-friendly Karl Johans Gate is a bustling street that offers a mix of high-end fashion boutiques, international brands, and local designer stores. For a more eclectic shopping experience, head to Grünerløkka, a trendy district known for its vintage shops, quirky boutiques, and vibrant markets.

2. Bergen: Known as the "Gateway to the Fjords," Bergen is a picturesque city with a rich history and a charming shopping scene. The historic Bryggen Wharf, a UNESCO World Heritage site, is lined with colourful wooden buildings housing souvenir shops, art galleries, and handicraft stores. Don't miss the famous fish market, where you can sample fresh seafood and pick up local specialties like dried fish and reindeer meat.

3. Trondheim: This mediaeval city combines old-world charm with modern shopping experiences. The vibrant Bakklandet neighbourhood features narrow cobblestone streets lined with boutique stores, antique shops, and quaint cafés. For a unique shopping experience,

visit the Trøndelag Folk Museum, where you can find traditional Norwegian crafts, textiles, and artwork.

4. Tromsø: Located in the Arctic Circle, Tromsø offers a distinctive shopping experience. The bustling city centre boasts a range of shops selling outdoor gear, winter clothing, and souvenirs. Explore Polaria, an Arctic-themed experience centre, which houses a gift shop with a wide selection of Arctic-inspired products and local handicrafts.

Dining in Norway:

1. Traditional Norwegian Cuisine: Norway's culinary scene is deeply rooted in its rich cultural heritage. Sample traditional dishes like lutefisk (dried fish), rakfisk (fermented fish), and reindeer stew. Don't forget to try Norwegian salmon, which is known for its exceptional quality. Many restaurants offer a "catch of the day" menu, showcasing fresh seafood from local waters.

2. New Nordic Cuisine: Norway has embraced the New Nordic Cuisine movement, focusing on fresh, locally sourced ingredients and innovative cooking techniques. Indulge in unique dining experiences

that celebrate the country's natural flavours and pristine landscapes. Look for restaurants that emphasise farm-to-table concepts and seasonal menus.

3. Street Food and Food Markets: Norway's cities offer a vibrant street food culture. Explore food markets such as Mathallen Oslo in Oslo and Bergen's Mathallen, where you can find a wide array of culinary delights, including artisanal cheeses, Nordic pastries, and international street food. Enjoy your meal in a lively atmosphere, surrounded by locals and fellow travellers.

4. Cafés and Bakeries: Norwegians have a deep appreciation for coffee and baked goods. Explore the cosy cafés scattered throughout the country, where you can savour freshly brewed coffee and indulge in delicious pastries like skillingsboller (cinnamon rolls) or krumkake (thin, waffle-like cookies).

Chapter 4. The Fjords of Western Norway

Bergen and the Gateway to the Fjords

Welcome to Bergen, the Gateway to the Fjords in Norway! Nestled on the southwestern coast of the country, Bergen is a charming city renowned for its stunning natural surroundings, rich cultural heritage, and vibrant atmosphere. Whether you're an outdoor enthusiast, a history buff, or a lover of arts and culture, Bergen has something to offer for everyone.

One of the main draws of Bergen is its proximity to the majestic Norwegian fjords. These deep, narrow inlets carved by glaciers offer breathtaking vistas of steep mountainsides, cascading waterfalls, and crystal-clear waters. From Bergen, you can embark on unforgettable fjord excursions, such as the popular Sognefjord, Hardangerfjord, or Nærøyfjord. Explore these picturesque landscapes by boat, kayak, or even on a scenic train journey that takes you through snow-capped peaks and verdant valleys.

Back in the city, Bergen's historic Bryggen Wharf is a UNESCO World Heritage site and a must-visit attraction. This iconic row of colorful wooden buildings dates back to the 14th century and once served as a hub for the Hanseatic League's trading activities. Take a stroll along the narrow alleyways, admire the traditional architecture, and discover charming boutiques, galleries, and cozy cafés tucked away in the nooks and crannies.

For panoramic views of Bergen and its surrounding fjords, hop on the Fløibanen funicular that transports you to the summit of Mount Fløyen. From here, you can enjoy sweeping vistas of the cityscape, mountains, and fjords below. It's also the perfect starting point for hiking trails that wind through the lush forests and offer a chance to connect with nature.

Culture enthusiasts will find plenty to explore in Bergen as well. The city is home to a vibrant arts scene, with numerous galleries, museums, and theaters. Visit the KODE Art Museums and Composer Homes to admire an extensive collection of Norwegian and international artworks, including pieces by Edvard Munch. The Bergen International Festival, held annually, showcases a diverse range of music, dance, and theater performances, attracting artists and spectators from around the world.

Food lovers won't be disappointed in Bergen either. Indulge in fresh seafood delicacies at the famous Fish Market, where you can sample locally caught fish, shellfish, and other Norwegian specialties. Don't forget to try the traditional Bergen fish soup, a creamy and flavorful dish that highlights the region's maritime heritage.

In summary, Bergen is a captivating destination that serves as the Gateway to the Fjords in Norway. With its breathtaking natural landscapes, historic charm, cultural treasures, and culinary delights, it offers an unforgettable experience for travelers seeking to immerse themselves in Norway's beauty and heritage.

Geirangerfjord

Geirangerfjord: A Norwegian Jewel

Nestled within the majestic landscapes of Norway, Geirangerfjord stands as an iconic natural wonder that captivates travelers from around the world. This breathtaking fjord, located in the southwestern part of the country, offers a picturesque blend of towering cliffs, cascading waterfalls, and serene waters that create an unparalleled sense of tranquility and awe.

As you embark on your journey to Geirangerfjord, prepare to be enveloped by a surreal atmosphere where nature's beauty reigns supreme. The fjord stretches for approximately 15 kilometers (9 miles) and is surrounded by steep mountains that rise over 1,400 meters (4,600 feet) above sea level, providing an awe-inspiring backdrop at every turn.

One of the most iconic features of Geirangerfjord is the Seven Sisters waterfall. This stunning cascade, consisting of seven distinct streams, descends from the mountain slopes and plunges dramatically into the fjord's pristine waters. The sight of this natural spectacle, accompanied by the sound of rushing water, is nothing short of mesmerizing.

For those seeking adventure, exploring Geirangerfjord by boat is an absolute must. Cruising along the calm waters, you'll have the opportunity to witness the fjord's grandeur up close. Marvel at the reflections of the mountains mirrored in the glassy surface, and feel the mist on your face as you glide past enchanting waterfalls such as the Bridal Veil and the Suitor. The experience is truly immersive, offering an unparalleled connection with nature.

To further immerse yourself in Geirangerfjord's allure, take a hike along the fjord's rim or venture up one of the surrounding mountains. The panoramic vistas from viewpoints like Dalsnibba and Flydalsjuvet are nothing short of extraordinary. These elevated vantage points allow you to witness the fjord's splendour from a different perspective, offering sweeping views that stretch as far as the eye can see.

Geiranger, a small village nestled at the head of the fjord, serves as a charming gateway to this natural wonder. Here, you can soak in the local culture, indulge in traditional Norwegian cuisine, and browse through shops showcasing handmade crafts and souvenirs. Don't forget to try the local delicacy of Geitost, a sweet and caramel-like goat cheese that is sure to tantalise your taste buds.

In addition to its natural allure, Geirangerfjord is also recognized as a UNESCO World Heritage site, affirming its exceptional universal value and the need for its preservation. The region's commitment to sustainability and responsible tourism ensures that future generations will continue to marvel at this stunning Norwegian jewel.

Whether you're an adventure seeker, a nature enthusiast, or simply someone yearning for a serene escape, Geirangerfjord beckons with its unrivalled beauty and tranquillity. Let the awe-inspiring landscapes and the symphony of nature's wonders enchant you as you explore this Norwegian gem, leaving you with memories that will last a lifetime.

Sognefjord

Welcome to the majestic Sognefjord, Norway's crown jewel of fjords! Renowned for its awe-inspiring beauty and enchanting landscapes, Sognefjord is a must-visit destination for nature lovers and adventure seekers alike. As the longest and deepest fjord in Norway, it stretches an impressive 205 kilometres (127 miles) inland, surrounded by towering mountains, cascading waterfalls, and charming villages.

One of the best ways to experience the grandeur of Sognefjord is by taking a scenic cruise along its crystal-clear waters. Board a ferry or a sightseeing boat, and immerse yourself in the breathtaking panoramas that unfold before your eyes. Admire the steep cliffs rising from the fjord, cloaked in verdant forests that paint the landscape with vibrant hues. Keep your camera ready to capture the magical moments as you sail past charming fishing villages nestled along the shoreline.

One of the most iconic spots along Sognefjord is Flåm, a small village embraced by towering mountains and cascading waterfalls. From here, you can embark on an unforgettable journey on the Flåm Railway, known as one of the world's most scenic train rides. The train ascends from the fjord's edge, twisting and turning through lush valleys, offering panoramic vistas of the fjord and its surrounding beauty.

If you're seeking a more active adventure, lace up your hiking boots and explore the numerous trails that weave through Sognefjord's dramatic landscapes. From gentle strolls to challenging hikes, there's something for everyone. Trek to viewpoints that offer awe-inspiring vistas, hike to glacier tongues, or wander through picturesque valleys dotted with grazing sheep and wildflowers.

History and culture enthusiasts will find ample opportunities to delve into the region's rich heritage. Visit the UNESCO-listed Nærøyfjord, an arm of Sognefjord known for its narrowness and dramatic landscapes. Explore the charming town of Bergen, once a thriving trading hub and gateway to the fjords. Wander through its historic Bryggen district, a UNESCO World Heritage site, and discover the remnants of its Hanseatic past.

To complete your Sognefjord experience, savour the local cuisine and indulge in the flavours of the sea. Freshly caught seafood, including salmon, trout, and cod, is a specialty of the region. Pair your meal with local delicacies like cloudberries or traditional brunost (brown cheese) for a true taste of Norway.

Whether you choose to cruise, hike, or immerse yourself in the cultural heritage, Sognefjord promises a journey of awe and wonder. Let the magnificence of this natural wonder leave an indelible mark on your travel memories, as you uncover the secrets and beauty of Norway's most breathtaking fjord.

Hardangerfjord

Welcome to the beautiful region of Hardangerfjord, nestled in the scenic country of Norway. Hardangerfjord is known for its breathtaking landscapes, crystal-clear waters, and charming cultural heritage. Whether you're a nature enthusiast, an adventure seeker, or a culture lover, this enchanting destination has something to offer everyone. Let's explore the wonders of Hardangerfjord together.

Hardangerfjord is Norway's second-longest fjord, stretching over 179 kilometres (111 miles) from the Atlantic Ocean into the heart of the Hardangervidda National Park. The fjord is famous for its dramatic cliffs, towering waterfalls, and lush green valleys, creating a picture-perfect setting that will leave you in awe.

One of the highlights of Hardangerfjord is the famous Trolltunga, a majestic rock formation that juts out horizontally over the fjord, offering an incredible vantage point for panoramic views. Hiking to Trolltunga is a popular adventure for outdoor enthusiasts, but be prepared for a challenging trek that rewards you with unforgettable vistas.

For a more leisurely experience, take a cruise along the fjord's calm waters, where you can marvel at the snow-capped peaks, cascading waterfalls, and picturesque fruit orchards that dot the landscape. The region is known for its thriving fruit cultivation, especially apples and cherries, and during the blooming season in spring, the fruit trees create a magical spectacle of colors.

To immerse yourself in the local culture, visit the charming villages that line the fjord. Norheimsund is a delightful town where you can explore the Hardanger Maritime Museum and learn about the area's rich seafaring history. Utne, one of the oldest villages in Hardanger, boasts a beautiful traditional hotel that has been welcoming visitors since the 17th century.

Nature lovers will find solace in the Hardangervidda National Park, a vast wilderness that is home to reindeer, arctic foxes, and numerous bird species. The park offers excellent hiking trails, fishing opportunities, and the chance to experience the untamed beauty of the Norwegian wilderness.

For those seeking a bit of adventure, try your hand at glacier hiking on the Folgefonna Glacier, an otherworldly ice expanse that stretches across 205 square kilometers (80 square miles). Guided tours allow you to explore the ice caves and crevasses while learning about the fascinating glacial landscape.

In addition to its natural wonders, Hardangerfjord hosts several annual events that showcase the local traditions and heritage. The Hardanger Music Festival and the Hardanger Fruit and Cider Festival are just a couple of examples where you can experience traditional music, dance, and indulge in delicious local produce.

To reach Hardangerfjord, the best way is by flying into Bergen, the gateway to the fjords. From Bergen, you can either rent a car or take public transportation to explore the region at your own pace. Alternatively, organized tours are available, providing a hassle-free way to discover the beauty of Hardangerfjord.

Hardangerfjord is a destination that captivates the hearts of travellers with its awe-inspiring landscapes, rich cultural heritage, and outdoor adventures. Whether you come to hike, cruise, or simply relax amidst nature's beauty, this Norwegian gem promises an unforgettable experience that will leave you with memories to last a lifetime.

Activities and Hiking Routes

Norway, with its breathtaking landscapes and diverse terrain, is a paradise for outdoor enthusiasts and hikers. From towering mountains and deep fjords to serene forests and picturesque valleys, this Nordic country offers a wide range of activities and hiking routes that will leave you awe-inspired. Here are some highlights to consider when planning your outdoor adventures in Norway.

1. Hiking in the Norwegian Fjords:
The Norwegian fjords are undoubtedly one of the country's most iconic and stunning natural features. Embark on a hiking expedition through the fjords to experience their grandeur up close. The Nærøyfjord, Geirangerfjord, and Sognefjord are among the most popular destinations for hikers. These fjords offer a variety of hiking routes, ranging from easy strolls along the shores to challenging treks up the surrounding peaks.

2. Trekking in Jotunheimen National Park:
Known as the "Home of the Giants," Jotunheimen National Park is a haven for mountaineers and hikers. It boasts Norway's highest mountains, including Galdhøpiggen, which stands at an impressive 2,469 meters (8,100 feet) above sea level. The park offers an extensive network of trails catering to all levels of hiking experience. The Besseggen Ridge, a popular hike, offers breathtaking views of the surrounding lakes and mountains.

3. Exploring the Lofoten Islands:

Located above the Arctic Circle, the Lofoten Islands offer a unique and awe-inspiring landscape. The jagged peaks, pristine beaches, and charming fishing villages make it a perfect destination for hiking enthusiasts. Explore trails such as Reinebringen, which rewards hikers with panoramic views over the iconic fishing village of Reine, or the hike to Mount Ryten for stunning vistas of Kvalvika Beach and the surrounding islands.

4. Discovering the Trolltunga:
Trolltunga, meaning "Troll's Tongue," is one of Norway's most famous and exhilarating hikes. Located in Hardangerfjord, this hike rewards adventurers with a breathtaking view from a cliff jutting out horizontally over 700 meters (2,300 feet) above Lake Ringedalsvatnet. The hike is challenging, covering approximately 23 kilometers (14 miles) round trip, and requires good physical fitness and preparation.

5. Walking the Romsdalseggen Ridge:
For those seeking a thrilling and panoramic hiking experience, the Romsdalseggen Ridge is a must-do. Situated in the Romsdal region, this hike offers stunning views of towering mountains, deep valleys, and the Romsdalsfjord. The trail spans

around 10 kilometres (6 miles) and features some exposed sections that require caution. Once you reach the end, you can descend into the valley via the famous Via Ferrata for an added adrenaline rush.

Remember, when embarking on any hiking adventure in Norway, it is crucial to be well-prepared and equipped with appropriate gear. Make sure to check weather conditions, bring plenty of water and food, and have a map or GPS device with you. Additionally, respect nature, follow designated trails, and leave no trace behind to preserve the pristine beauty of Norway's wilderness. Happy hiking!

Chapter 5. Northern Norway and the Arctic

Tromsø and the Midnight Sun

Welcome to Tromsø, a captivating city located in the breathtaking region of Northern Norway. Known as the "Gateway to the Arctic," Tromsø is a vibrant and picturesque destination that offers a unique experience, especially during the magical phenomenon of the Midnight Sun.

Tromsø is situated above the Arctic Circle, which means it enjoys the phenomena of the Midnight Sun during the summer months. From late May to mid-July, the sun remains above the horizon, casting its warm, golden light throughout the day and night. This natural phenomenon creates an otherworldly atmosphere, providing visitors with an unforgettable experience.

The Midnight Sun offers a myriad of opportunities for exploration and outdoor activities. Imagine hiking under the glowing sun at 2 a.m., kayaking through tranquil fjords bathed in a soft, ethereal light, or simply savouring a cup of coffee at a local café while the sun hangs high in the sky at midnight. The extended daylight hours allow you to make the most of your time, indulging in endless adventures and creating lasting memories.

One of the best ways to immerse yourself in the Midnight Sun experience is by embarking on a scenic cruise or boat tour. Tromsø's pristine coastal landscapes, dotted with islands, fjords, and snow-capped mountains, provide a stunning backdrop for your journey. Capture breathtaking photographs of the glowing sun reflecting off calm waters, and keep an eye out for wildlife like seals, whales, and seabirds that thrive in these Arctic waters.

For those seeking a more active experience, hiking in Tromsø's surrounding mountains and trails is an absolute must. The Tromsdalstinden peak, standing majestically at 1,238 metres, offers a challenging but rewarding climb, with panoramic views that will leave you in awe. During the Midnight Sun period, you can embark on hikes at any time of day, immersing yourself in the enchanting beauty of the Arctic landscape.

To fully embrace Tromsø's Midnight Sun, don't miss the opportunity to join a summer festival or cultural event. The city comes alive during this time, with concerts, outdoor markets, and various celebrations taking place. The Midnight Sun Marathon, a popular event among locals and visitors alike, allows participants to run under the golden glow of the sun during the late evening hours.

As the night sky never truly darkens, Tromsø also offers fantastic opportunities for stargazing and witnessing the mystical phenomenon of the Northern Lights, even during the summer months. Imagine the ethereal dance of colourful lights against the backdrop of the glowing sun, an experience that defies the boundaries of imagination.

Whether you're a nature enthusiast, adventure seeker, or simply captivated by the wonders of the natural world, Tromsø and it's Midnight Sun are sure to leave an indelible mark on your travel memories. Explore this enchanting destination and create lifelong memories while basking in the ethereal beauty of the Arctic summer.

Lofoten Islands

Welcome to the stunning Lofoten Islands, a picturesque archipelago situated off the northwestern coast of Norway. Renowned for their dramatic landscapes, rugged mountains, pristine beaches, and vibrant fishing villages, the Lofoten Islands offer an unforgettable travel experience.

Whether you're an outdoor enthusiast, a photography enthusiast, or simply seeking tranquillity in nature, this breathtaking destination has something for everyone.

Getting There:
The Lofoten Islands are accessible by air and sea. The closest airport is Leknes Airport, located on Vestvågøy Island, which receives domestic flights from major cities in Norway. Alternatively, you can fly to Evenes Airport, Harstad/Narvik, and then take a scenic bus or car journey to reach the islands. If you prefer travelling by sea, there are ferry connections from Bodø to Moskenes or Svolvær, providing a picturesque voyage through the Norwegian fjords.

Natural Beauty:
The Lofoten Islands are renowned for their majestic natural beauty. The archipelago is characterised by towering granite peaks, deep fjords, pristine white sandy beaches, and crystal-clear turquoise waters. One of the most iconic sights is the dramatic Lofoten Wall, a series of towering mountains that rise dramatically from the sea. The islands offer numerous hiking trails, including the famous Reinebringen and Mannen hikes, providing

breathtaking panoramic views of the surrounding landscapes.

Vibrant Fishing Villages:
The Lofoten Islands are dotted with charming fishing villages that exude a unique charm. One of the most picturesque villages is Reine, known for its idyllic location nestled between towering mountains and pristine waters. Wander through the narrow streets lined with traditional red and yellow fisherman's cabins called "rorbuer" and soak in the laid-back atmosphere. You can also visit Nusfjord, a well-preserved fishing village dating back to the 19th century, or Henningsvær, an artsy village with vibrant galleries and charming cafes.

Outdoor Activities:
Adventure seekers will find plenty of activities to indulge in while visiting the Lofoten Islands. The archipelago is a haven for hiking, climbing, and kayaking enthusiasts. Embark on a kayaking tour to explore the fjords and admire the wildlife, including seals, otters, and seabirds. Fishing is also a popular activity here, and you can join a local fishing excursion to experience the thrill of catching your own dinner. During winter, the Lofoten Islands transform into a winter wonderland, attracting avid

skiers and offering opportunities for snowshoeing and Northern Lights hunting.

Cultural Experiences:
Immerse yourself in the local culture of the Lofoten Islands by visiting the various museums and art galleries. The Lofoten Museum in Kabelvåg showcases the region's rich history, including the traditional fishing industry, while the Espolin Gallery in Kabelvåg exhibits contemporary art inspired by the Arctic landscapes. Don't miss the chance to try the local cuisine, especially the renowned dried fish known as "stockfish," which has been a staple of the local diet for centuries.

Conclusion:
The Lofoten Islands in Norway offer a captivating blend of natural beauty, outdoor adventures, and cultural experiences. From awe-inspiring landscapes to vibrant fishing villages and a plethora of outdoor activities, this archipelago promises an unforgettable journey for travelers seeking an escape into the untouched wonders of nature. So pack your bags and get ready to explore the breathtaking Lofoten Islands, where every moment is a postcard-worthy memory.

North Cape

Welcome to North Cape, a captivating destination nestled in the northernmost reaches of Norway. Renowned for its dramatic landscapes, breathtaking views, and unique Arctic experiences, North Cape is a must-visit location for intrepid travellers seeking adventure and natural beauty.

1. Discover the Northernmost Point of Europe:
At North Cape, you'll have the opportunity to stand at the northernmost point of mainland Europe, where the vast expanse of the Arctic Ocean stretches before you. This iconic landmark offers an incredible sense of awe and achievement, as you gaze out into the endless horizon, surrounded by rugged cliffs and Arctic tundra.

2. Witness the Midnight Sun:
One of the most extraordinary phenomena in the North Cape is the midnight sun. During the summer months, the sun remains visible above the horizon for 24 hours a day, casting an ethereal glow over the landscape. It's a surreal experience to witness the golden hues of the midnight sun, providing ample opportunities for unforgettable photography and endless outdoor activities, even at the darkest hour.

3. Explore the Arctic Wilderness:
North Cape is a gateway to a pristine Arctic wilderness, where you can immerse yourself in nature's grandeur. Embark on hiking trails that wind through dramatic cliffs, ancient valleys, and moss-covered landscapes. Marvel at the vibrant flora and fauna, including reindeer herds, Arctic foxes, and seabird colonies. The silence and solitude of the Arctic wilderness offer a peaceful retreat from the hustle and bustle of daily life.

4. Chasing the Northern Lights:
For those seeking the celestial magic of the Northern Lights, North Cape is an ideal destination. Away from light pollution, you'll have a higher chance of witnessing nature's most dazzling light show. Be prepared to be spellbound as shimmering ribbons of green, blue, and purple dance across the Arctic sky, creating a spectacle that will leave you in awe.

5. Rich Cultural Heritage:
North Cape is not just a place of natural wonders; it also boasts a rich cultural heritage. Visit the North Cape Museum to learn about the history and traditions of the indigenous Sami people, who have thrived in this Arctic region for centuries. Discover

their unique way of life, traditional crafts, and reindeer herding practices.

6. Arctic Adventures:
North Cape offers a wide array of exciting activities for adventurous souls. Embark on a thrilling snowmobile safari, go dog sledding through pristine snowy landscapes, or try your hand at ice fishing. During the summer, you can engage in activities like kayaking, birdwatching, and even whale watching, as humpback and killer whales migrate through these Arctic waters.

7. Warm Hospitality and Authentic Cuisine:
While exploring the North Cape, take the opportunity to indulge in the region's authentic cuisine. Try traditional dishes like reindeer meat, Arctic char, and king crab, which reflect the local flavours and culinary traditions. Don't miss the chance to warm up in cosy local restaurants and enjoy the warm hospitality of the people who call this remote region home.

North Cape is a place where nature's grandeur meets the Arctic mystique. From standing at the edge of the world to witnessing awe-inspiring natural phenomena, this destination offers a truly unforgettable experience. Immerse yourself in the raw beauty of North Cape, and let its Arctic charm captivate your senses.

Sami Culture and Reindeer Sledding

Sami culture and reindeer sledding are closely intertwined traditions in Norway. The Sami people, also known as Sámi or Saami, are the indigenous inhabitants of the northern regions of Norway, Sweden, Finland, and parts of Russia. Reindeer sledding is a significant aspect of their cultural heritage and plays a vital role in their traditional way of life.

The Sami people have a deep connection with nature and rely on reindeer herding for their livelihood. Reindeer herding is not only a means of subsistence but also a central element of their cultural identity. It involves the seasonal migration of reindeer herds between their winter and summer grazing areas, known as winter pastures and summer pastures.

Reindeer sledding, or "joiking," is the traditional mode of transportation used by the Sami people in the Arctic regions. It involves a sled or sleigh pulled by reindeer. The Sami have perfected the art of reindeer sledding over generations, developing specific techniques and equipment suited for the harsh Arctic environment. Reindeer sleds are typically made of wood, and the reindeer are harnessed to the sled using leather straps.

Reindeer sledding offers an immersive experience that allows visitors to explore the Arctic wilderness and gain insights into the Sami way of life. In Norway, several Sami communities provide reindeer sledding tours for tourists who wish to experience this unique cultural tradition. These tours often take place in remote, pristine areas where visitors can witness the stunning natural beauty of the Arctic landscape while being pulled by a team of reindeer.

During the sledding tours, visitors can learn about the Sami culture, traditions, and the symbiotic relationship between the Sami people and their reindeer. Sami guides often share their knowledge about reindeer herding, traditional storytelling, and the significance of reindeer in their daily lives. It's an opportunity to gain a deeper understanding of Sami history, customs, and the challenges they face in preserving their cultural heritage.

Reindeer sledding tours are typically available during the winter months when the Arctic landscape is covered in snow, creating perfect conditions for sledding. However, it's important to note that these tours should be approached with respect for the Sami people and their way of life. It's crucial to choose responsible tour operators who prioritise sustainable and ethical practices, ensuring the well-being of the reindeer and the preservation of Sami culture.

In recent years, there has been a growing appreciation for Sami culture and reindeer sledding among both locals and international visitors. It is seen as a way to promote cultural diversity, support indigenous communities, and foster a greater understanding of the Arctic environment. The combination of stunning natural beauty, immersive cultural experiences, and the thrill of reindeer sledding make it a truly unforgettable adventure in Norway's Arctic regions.

Northern Lights Viewing

Northern Lights viewing in Norway is an awe-inspiring and unforgettable experience for travellers from around the world. Norway's proximity to the Arctic Circle makes it one of the prime locations to witness the magical dance of the Aurora Borealis, also known as the Northern Lights.

The best time to see the Northern Lights in Norway is during the winter months, from late September to early April. The long nights and clear, dark skies create ideal conditions for viewing this natural phenomenon. It's important to note that the Northern Lights are a natural occurrence and can never be guaranteed, but Norway offers some of the highest chances of seeing them.

There are several locations in Norway that are renowned for their Northern Lights displays. Tromsø, often referred to as the "Gateway to the Arctic," is one of the most popular destinations. It has excellent infrastructure and a range of activities to offer, making it a great base for Northern Lights enthusiasts. Tromsø's surrounding areas, such as the Lyngen Alps and the island of Senja, provide stunning backdrops for the light show.

Another sought-after destination is the Lofoten Islands. With their picturesque landscapes, including rugged mountains, fjords, and pristine beaches, the Lofoten Islands offer a unique setting for Northern Lights viewing. The islands' remote location and lack of light pollution enhance the chances of witnessing a dazzling display.

For those seeking a more off-the-beaten-path experience, the Finnmark region in northern Norway is worth considering. It's sparsely populated and boasts vast wilderness areas, which make for exceptional Northern Lights viewing opportunities. Places like Alta and Kirkenes in Finnmark offer various accommodations and activities tailored to aurora hunters.

To enhance the experience, many tour operators in Norway provide guided Northern Lights tours. These tours often include transportation, expert guides who are knowledgeable about the science and folklore surrounding the lights, warm clothing, and hot beverages to keep you comfortable during the chilly nights. Some tours even offer unique experiences like dog sledding or snowmobiling under the Northern Lights.

Remember, the Northern Lights are a natural phenomenon, and their visibility depends on several factors. Clear skies, low light pollution, and strong solar activity increase the chances of witnessing a vibrant display. It's advisable to check the weather forecasts and aurora activity predictions before planning your trip to maximize the chances of seeing the Northern Lights.

In conclusion, Norway provides an excellent opportunity to witness the enchanting dance of the Northern Lights. With its stunning landscapes, remote locations, and infrastructure designed for aurora enthusiasts, Norway is a dream destination for anyone seeking a memorable Northern Lights experience.

Chapter 6. Coastal Gems and Islands

Ålesund and Art Nouveau Architecture

Ålesund is a picturesque coastal town located on the western coast of Norway. It is known for its stunning Art Nouveau architecture and breathtaking natural surroundings. The town holds a special place in Norway's architectural history and is often referred to as the Art Nouveau capital of the country.

Ålesund's unique architectural style can be attributed to a devastating fire that swept through the town in 1904. The fire destroyed most of the original wooden buildings, leading to a massive reconstruction effort. The town was rebuilt in the Art Nouveau style, which was prevalent in Europe at the time, resulting in an enchanting blend of Norwegian and continental influences.

Art Nouveau, also known as Jugendstil or "youth style," emerged as a reaction against the industrialization and mass production of the late 19th century. It emphasised craftsmanship, intricate ornamentation, and organic forms inspired by nature. In Ålesund, this architectural style took shape in the form of vibrant facades, intricate detailing, and imaginative ornamentation.

The buildings in Ålesund feature characteristic elements of Art Nouveau, such as asymmetrical designs, curved lines, floral motifs, and delicate ironwork. The facades are adorned with decorative elements like stylized flowers, leaves, and mythical creatures, showcasing the creativity and craftsmanship of the architects and artisans involved in the reconstruction.

One of the prominent architects responsible for Ålesund's Art Nouveau transformation was Ålesund's own resident architect, Hagbarth Schytte-Berg. He played a crucial role in designing several iconic buildings, including the Hotel Brosundet, the Apoteker Target, and the Jugendstilsenteret (Art Nouveau Center). The Jugendstilsenteret, housed in the former Swan Pharmacy building, serves as a museum and documentation centre dedicated to the history and preservation of Art Nouveau.

The location of Ålesund adds to its allure. Situated on several islands at the entrance of the iconic Geirangerfjord, the town offers breathtaking views of the surrounding mountains, fjords, and the Norwegian Sea. Visitors can explore the narrow streets, stroll along the scenic waterfront, and admire the intricate architectural details that adorn the buildings.

The combination of Ålesund's captivating Art Nouveau architecture, stunning natural landscapes, and maritime heritage makes it a popular tourist destination in Norway. Visitors can delve into the town's history, explore museums, enjoy boat trips to nearby islands and fjords, and indulge in delicious seafood from local restaurants.

Overall, Ålesund stands as a testament to the resilience of its inhabitants and their commitment to preserving their cultural heritage. The town's Art Nouveau architecture serves as a living testament to the craftsmanship and artistic expression of a bygone era, captivating visitors with its timeless beauty.

Trondheim and Nidaros Cathedral

Trondheim and Nidaros Cathedral are not located in Nigeria. Trondheim is a city in Norway, specifically in the central part of the country. Meanwhile, Nidaros Cathedral, also known as Nidarosdomen, is a prominent landmark and the largest mediaeval building in Norway, located in Trondheim.

Trondheim, historically known as Nidaros, is the third-largest city in Norway and has a rich cultural and historical heritage. It was founded in the 11th century and served as the capital of Norway during the Viking Age and the Middle Ages. Today, Trondheim is a vibrant city known for its picturesque surroundings, charming wooden buildings, and a blend of modern and traditional architecture.

Nidaros Cathedral, located in Trondheim, holds great significance in Norwegian history and is considered the national sanctuary of Norway. The construction of the cathedral began in the 11th century and continued over several centuries, resulting in a stunning example of Gothic architecture. It is particularly famous for its intricate stained glass windows, intricate wood carvings, and beautiful sculptures. Nidaros Cathedral is closely associated with the history of the Norwegian monarchy and has served as the site of coronations and royal weddings.

While Trondheim and Nidaros Cathedral are not located in Nigeria, both places have a unique cultural and historical significance in Norway. Trondheim offers visitors a chance to explore the country's mediaeval past, enjoy scenic landscapes, and immerse themselves in Norwegian culture. Nidaros Cathedral stands as a symbol of national identity and remains an important pilgrimage site for both locals and tourists.

The Atlantic Road

The Atlantic Road, also known as Atlanterhavsveien in Norwegian, is a stunning scenic road located along the Norwegian coastline. It is renowned as one of the most picturesque drives in the world, attracting thousands of visitors each year. The road stretches across a series of small islands and skerries, connecting the municipalities of Averøy and Eide in the Møre og Romsdal county of Norway.

The Atlantic Road spans approximately 8.3 kilometres (5.2 miles) and is a remarkable feat of engineering. It winds its way through a captivating landscape of rocky shores, islets, and the vast expanse of the Atlantic Ocean. The road consists of eight bridges, including the iconic Storseisundet Bridge, which curves dramatically over the sea, giving the impression of a road that leads straight into the ocean. This unique design has made the Atlantic Road a symbol of Norwegian engineering ingenuity.

The road offers breathtaking views from every angle, with the ever-changing weather and the roaring waves of the Atlantic Ocean providing a dramatic backdrop. On calm days, the water reflects the surrounding landscape, creating a mesmerising mirror effect. Stormy weather can also be a thrilling experience, as powerful waves crash against the sturdy bridges, creating a spectacle that draws photographers and nature enthusiasts.

Driving along the Atlantic Road is an exhilarating adventure. The road twists and turns, offering scenic viewpoints and rest areas where visitors can stop and admire the beauty of the Norwegian coastline. It is particularly popular among road trip enthusiasts, motorcyclists, and cyclists who appreciate the serenity and grandeur of the surroundings.

Aside from the stunning natural scenery, the Atlantic Road is also home to diverse marine life. Fishing is a common activity in the area, and visitors can catch fish such as cod, pollock, and mackerel. The road itself has been designated as a national tourist route, with several attractions and facilities along the way, including fishing spots, picnic areas, and restaurants serving fresh seafood.

The best time to visit the Atlantic Road is during the summer months, when the weather is generally milder and the days are longer. However, it is important to note that the weather along the Norwegian coastline can be unpredictable, so it's advisable to check the forecast and plan accordingly.

In conclusion, the Atlantic Road in Norway is a remarkable scenic route that offers a memorable and awe-inspiring journey. With its breathtaking views, impressive bridges, and proximity to the majestic Atlantic Ocean, it is no wonder that the Atlantic Road has become an iconic destination for travelers seeking natural beauty and an unforgettable road trip experience.

Røros Mining Town

Røros Mining Town is a historic town located in Norway, specifically in Trøndelag county. It is renowned for its unique and well-preserved mining heritage, earning it a place on the UNESCO World Heritage List in 1980. Røros Mining Town holds significant historical, cultural, and architectural value, making it a popular tourist destination.

The town's history dates back to the 17th century when copper ore was discovered in the region. The mining operations started in 1644 and continued for over 300 years, until 1977. During its peak, Røros was one of the most important mining towns in Norway and a significant supplier of copper to Europe.

The mining operations greatly influenced the development of the town and its surrounding areas. Røros Mining Town features a unique combination of traditional Scandinavian architecture and wooden buildings. The buildings, painted in a distinctive red colour, create a charming and picturesque atmosphere. The town's layout and infrastructure were designed to support the mining operations, with the streets and buildings carefully planned and organised.

The Røros Copper Works, located in the heart of the town, served as the main hub for mining activities. The works consisted of various buildings, including smelters, foundries, and warehouses, all essential for the extraction and processing of copper. Today, these structures stand as a testament to the town's industrial past.

Aside from the mining operations, Røros Mining Town also had a unique social structure. Miners and their families lived in well-defined districts called "gårds," where each family had their own house and land for farming. This system helped foster a strong sense of community among the residents.

Exploring Røros Mining Town today offers visitors a glimpse into its rich history. The town has an open-air museum called Røros Museum, which showcases the mining heritage and provides insights into the lives of the people who lived and worked there. The museum exhibits mining tools, artefacts, and displays that depict the town's social and cultural aspects.

Furthermore, Røros hosts several cultural events throughout the year, attracting both locals and tourists. The most notable event is the Røros Winter Fair, held annually since 1854. During the fair, the town comes alive with various activities, including markets, exhibitions, concerts, and traditional performances.

The natural surroundings of Røros Mining Town are also worth exploring. The region offers opportunities for outdoor activities like hiking, skiing, and fishing. The rolling hills, forests, and lakes provide a scenic backdrop to the historical town.

In conclusion, Røros Mining Town in Norway is a remarkable destination that combines historical significance, cultural heritage, and natural beauty. Its well-preserved mining heritage, unique architecture, and community structure make it an enchanting place to visit for history enthusiasts, architecture lovers, and those seeking an authentic Norwegian experience.

Islands of Southern Norway

The islands of Southern Norway are a picturesque and diverse archipelago that stretches along the country's southern coastline. With their stunning landscapes, rich cultural heritage, and abundant natural beauty, these islands offer a unique and captivating experience for visitors.

One of the most well-known island groups in Southern Norway is the Southern Archipelago, which includes hundreds of islands, islets, and skerries. The largest islands in this group are Aust-Agder and Vest-Agder, each with its own distinct charm and attractions. The Southern Archipelago is known for its idyllic coastal villages, pristine beaches, and crystal-clear waters. It's a popular destination for boating, fishing, and outdoor activities, where visitors can explore hidden coves, go kayaking, or simply relax in the serene surroundings.

Another remarkable island in Southern Norway is the picturesque Lindesnes Island, located at the southernmost point of the Norwegian mainland. Lindesnes is renowned for its historic lighthouse, which has guided ships along the treacherous Norwegian coastline for centuries. The lighthouse offers breathtaking views of the surrounding ocean and is a popular spot for tourists to visit.

Moving further west, we come across the enchanting islands of Lista and Jomfruland. Lista, located in Vest-Agder County, is known for its stunning beaches and sand dunes, making it a paradise for sun-seekers and nature enthusiasts. Jomfruland, on the other hand, is part of the Telemark region and is famous for its diverse birdlife, nature reserves, and beautiful cycling routes.

If you're looking for a taste of maritime history, a visit to the island of Hydra is a must. Situated in the Flekkefjord municipality, Hidra is a quaint island with well-preserved wooden houses, narrow streets, and a rich seafaring heritage. Its charming atmosphere and scenic landscapes make it a perfect spot for those seeking tranquillity and a glimpse into Norway's past.

Beyond these islands, there are countless other hidden gems scattered along the southern coast of Norway. Whether you're looking for vibrant cultural festivals, outdoor adventures, or simply a peaceful retreat surrounded by nature, the islands of Southern Norway offer a wide range of experiences to suit every taste.

In conclusion, the islands of Southern Norway are a treasure trove of natural beauty, cultural heritage, and outdoor activities. From the Southern Archipelago to Lindesnes, Lista, Jomfruland, Hidra, and beyond, these islands provide an unforgettable journey through Norway's coastal wonders. Whether you're a nature lover, history enthusiast, or adventure seeker, Southern Norway's islands are sure to captivate you with their charm and allure.

Chapter 7. Outdoor Adventures

Hiking and Trekking Routes

Norway is renowned for its stunning natural landscapes, including majestic mountains, deep fjords, and pristine wilderness. It offers a plethora of hiking and trekking routes that cater to both beginners and experienced outdoor enthusiasts. Here are some notable routes in Norway:

1. Pulpit Rock (Preikestolen): Located in southwestern Norway near Stavanger, Pulpit Rock is one of the country's most iconic hikes. The trail takes you to a flat plateau perched 604 meters above the Lysefjord, providing breathtaking panoramic views.

2. Trolltunga: Situated in the Hardangerfjord region, Trolltunga (Troll's Tongue) is another famous hiking destination. The 22-kilometre round-trip trail leads to a dramatic rock formation jutting out over Lake Ringedalsvatnet, offering awe-inspiring views. It's a challenging hike, but the reward is well worth it.

3. Besseggen Ridge: Located in Jotunheimen National Park, Besseggen is a classic trekking route known for its spectacular views. The trail follows a

narrow ridge between the Gjende and Bessvatnet lakes, offering stunning vistas of the surrounding peaks and glaciers.

4. Romsdalseggen Ridge: Situated in the Romsdal Alps near Åndalsnes, this ridge hike provides breathtaking views of the Romsdalen Valley, fjords, and surrounding mountains. The 10.3-kilometer trail offers a mix of steep ascents, narrow paths, and exposed sections.

5. Jotunheimen National Park: As Norway's premier mountainous region, Jotunheimen offers a wide range of hiking and trekking opportunities. From day hikes to multi-day adventures, you can explore numerous trails that traverse glaciers, cross high mountain passes, and lead to picturesque lakes and peaks.

6. Hardangervidda National Park: Known as Europe's largest mountain plateau, Hardangervidda offers vast wilderness and unique hiking experiences. The park boasts numerous trails, including the famous four-day hike from Finse to Haukeliseter, passing through diverse landscapes and showcasing the beauty of the Norwegian wilderness.

7. Kjerag: Located in southern Norway near Lysefjord, Kjerag is a challenging hike that rewards hikers with stunning views and a chance to stand on the famous Kjerag Boulder—a massive rock wedged between two cliffs. It's a demanding trail that requires proper preparation and experience.

These are just a few examples of the incredible hiking and trekking routes available in Norway. It's essential to plan your hikes carefully, considering weather conditions, trail difficulty, and safety precautions. Norway's outdoor culture and stunning landscapes make it a dream destination for hiking and trekking enthusiasts.

Wildlife Safaris

Wildlife safaris in Norway offer a unique and thrilling experience for nature enthusiasts and animal lovers. Norway is known for its breathtaking landscapes, pristine wilderness, and diverse range of wildlife species. From majestic polar bears to reindeer herds, there is a wide variety of animals that can be observed in their natural habitat during a wildlife safari in Norway.

One of the most popular destinations for wildlife safaris in Norway is Svalbard, an archipelago located in the Arctic Ocean. Svalbard is home to polar bears, which are the largest land predators in the world. These safaris typically involve guided tours on specialised vehicles or snowmobiles, allowing visitors to observe polar bears from a safe distance. It's an awe-inspiring experience to witness these magnificent creatures in their icy surroundings.

Another iconic wildlife species in Norway is the mighty Norwegian elk, also known as the moose. The country's vast forests provide the perfect habitat for these impressive animals. Wildlife safaris focused on moose often take place in areas such as Hedmark and Trøndelag, where visitors can embark on guided tours or even spend a night in a wildlife hide to observe these majestic creatures up close.

In addition to polar bears and moose, Norway is home to numerous other fascinating animals. The country's fjords and coastal regions offer excellent opportunities for whale watching safaris. Species such as humpback whales, orcas, and fin whales can often be spotted during boat excursions in places like Tromsø and Andenes. Bird enthusiasts will also appreciate the diverse birdlife found in Norway, including sea eagles, puffins, and various species of owls.

To ensure the welfare of the animals and preserve their natural habitat, wildlife safaris in Norway are typically conducted in a responsible and sustainable manner. Experienced guides and tour operators prioritise the well-being of the animals and educate visitors about conservation efforts. It is crucial to respect the animals' space and follow strict guidelines to minimise disturbance and maintain a positive impact on the environment.

Norway's wildlife safaris provide an opportunity to connect with nature, witness incredible wildlife spectacles, and gain a deeper understanding of the country's rich natural heritage. Whether you are seeking encounters with polar bears, moose, whales, or birds, Norway's diverse ecosystems and well-regulated safari experiences offer a truly unforgettable adventure for wildlife enthusiasts of all ages.

Skiing and Winter Sports

Norway, with its breathtaking landscapes and snow-capped mountains, is a paradise for winter sports enthusiasts. Skiing in Norway is an exhilarating experience that combines stunning natural beauty with thrilling adventure. Whether you're a seasoned skier or a novice looking to learn,

Norway offers a wide range of ski resorts and winter activities to suit all skill levels.

One of the most popular destinations for skiing in Norway is the region of Hemsedal. Known as the "Scandinavian Alps," Hemsedal boasts some of the best ski slopes in the country. With over 50 kilometers of downhill slopes and a variety of off-piste terrain, skiers of all abilities can find their perfect run. The resort also offers well-groomed cross-country ski trails for those who prefer a more tranquil experience.

Another renowned ski destination in Norway is Trysil, located in the eastern part of the country. Trysil is Scandinavia's largest ski resort and features an impressive network of slopes, totaling over 70 kilometers in length. The resort caters to skiers and snowboarders of all ages and skill levels, with gentle slopes for beginners and challenging black runs for advanced skiers. Trysil also offers a range of family-friendly activities, including snow parks and dedicated children's areas.

For a truly unique skiing experience, head to the western region of Norway and explore the famous Fjord Norway. The iconic fjords, surrounded by majestic mountains, create a stunning backdrop for your skiing adventures. Resorts such as Voss and Geilo offer a mix of downhill and cross-country skiing opportunities, allowing you to immerse yourself in the breathtaking scenery while enjoying your favourite winter sport.

If you're seeking a more off-the-beaten-path skiing experience, consider visiting the lesser-known resorts of Røldal and Myrkdalen. Røldal is renowned for its abundant snowfall, making it a haven for powder enthusiasts. The resort features challenging off-piste terrain and is a popular destination for freeride skiing and snowboarding. Myrkdalen, on the other hand, is perfect for families and beginners, with wide, gentle slopes and excellent ski schools.

In addition to downhill skiing, Norway offers a range of other winter activities. Cross-country skiing is a beloved national pastime, with countless kilometres of well-maintained trails crisscrossing the country. Snowshoeing, ice climbing, and dog sledding are also popular options for those seeking alternative winter adventures.

Norway's winter sports scene is not just limited to skiing. The country has produced numerous world-class athletes in disciplines such as ski jumping, biathlon, and cross-country skiing. Visitors can witness the excitement of these sports by attending local competitions and events, which often draw large crowds of enthusiastic spectators.

When planning a ski trip to Norway, it's important to come prepared with appropriate clothing and equipment. The weather conditions can be variable, so layering is key to staying warm and comfortable. It's also worth noting that daylight hours are limited during the winter months, particularly in the northern regions, so it's advisable to make the most of the daylight and plan your activities accordingly.

Norway's ski resorts offer a wide range of accommodations, from cosy cabins and traditional lodges to modern hotels with spa facilities. Many resorts also provide ski-in/ski-out access, allowing you to hit the slopes right from your doorstep. After a day of skiing, unwind in a sauna, indulge in local cuisine at mountain restaurants, or simply relax and enjoy the stunning views.

With its majestic mountains, pristine snow, and well-developed winter sports infrastructure, Norway is an ideal destination for skiing and winter sports enthusiasts. Whether you're seeking thrilling downhill runs, peaceful cross-country trails, or unique winter adventures, Norway has it all.

Fishing and Sailing

Fishing and sailing in Norway are popular activities that offer unique and rewarding experiences for both locals and tourists. Norway's extensive coastline, fjords, and rich marine ecosystems make it an ideal destination for fishing enthusiasts and sailing aficionados alike.

Norway is known for its abundance of fish species, including Atlantic salmon, cod, haddock, halibut, and trout, among others. Anglers from around the world are attracted to Norway's pristine rivers, lakes, and coastal waters for their exceptional fishing opportunities. The country's strict fishing regulations ensure the sustainability of its fisheries, making it a prime location for catch-and-release practices or for those looking to enjoy a delicious fresh fish meal.

One of the most popular fishing destinations in Norway is the Lofoten Islands, located above the Arctic Circle. Lofoten offers stunning landscapes with towering mountains, picturesque villages, and crystal-clear waters teeming with fish. Visitors can try their luck with sea fishing or venture into the numerous lakes and rivers to catch salmon or trout. The midnight sun during the summer months provides extended fishing hours and a unique atmosphere.

Sailing is another fantastic way to explore Norway's breathtaking coastline and fjords. Norway's coastline stretches over 25,000 kilometres, offering countless opportunities for sailors to navigate through narrow passages, scenic archipelagos, and deep fjords surrounded by towering cliffs. The fjords, such as the famous Geirangerfjord and Sognefjord, provide a stunning backdrop for a sailing adventure.

Sailors in Norway can also enjoy the challenge of navigating open waters and experiencing the unique weather conditions of the North Atlantic. The coastal waters offer a mix of calm sailing conditions and more challenging stretches with stronger winds and waves, making it a diverse and exciting experience for sailors of all levels.

Norway's vibrant maritime culture is deeply rooted in its history and traditions. Along the coast, you'll find numerous fishing villages and towns where you can witness the traditional fishing lifestyle and learn about the local heritage. Many fishing communities also offer opportunities for visitors to join fishing excursions or learn traditional fishing techniques.

In recent years, there has been a rise in eco-friendly and sustainable tourism practices in Norway, including fishing and sailing. Visitors are encouraged to respect the natural environment, follow fishing regulations, and minimize their impact on the delicate ecosystems. This ensures that future generations can continue to enjoy the pristine beauty of Norway's waters.

Whether you're an avid angler or a sailing enthusiast, Norway provides an unparalleled experience for fishing and sailing. The combination of breathtaking landscapes, diverse marine life, and rich cultural heritage makes it a dream destination for those seeking outdoor adventures on the water.

Camping and National Parks

Camping and national parks in Norway offer incredible opportunities for outdoor enthusiasts and nature lovers. Norway's breathtaking landscapes, rugged mountains, pristine fjords, and abundant wildlife make it a perfect destination for camping and exploring its national parks.

Norway is home to numerous national parks, each with its own unique features and natural wonders. Some of the most popular national parks for camping include Jotunheimen National Park, Rondane National Park, Hardangervidda National Park, and Dovrefjell-Sunndalsfjella National Park, among others. These parks offer a wide range of activities such as hiking, fishing, canoeing, wildlife spotting, and, of course, camping.

Camping in Norway's national parks is a fantastic way to immerse yourself in the stunning wilderness and experience the country's natural beauty up close. There are designated campsites available in most national parks, ranging from basic tent sites to more developed areas with amenities like toilets, fire pits, and picnic areas. These campsites are generally well-maintained and provide a peaceful setting for enjoying the outdoors.

One popular activity while camping in Norway is hiking. The national parks offer an extensive network of well-marked trails that cater to hikers of all skill levels. Whether you're a novice or an experienced trekker, you can find trails that suit your abilities and preferences. Hiking in Norway allows you to witness awe-inspiring landscapes, including majestic mountains, glaciers, waterfalls, and stunning viewpoints.

Fishing is another popular pastime in Norway's national parks, thanks to the country's abundance of lakes, rivers, and coastal areas. Many of the parks have fishing opportunities, and you can try your hand at catching trout, salmon, Arctic char, or other species. However, it's important to familiarize yourself with local regulations and obtain the necessary permits before fishing in these areas.

Wildlife enthusiasts will be delighted by the diverse fauna found in Norway's national parks. The parks are home to a range of species, including reindeer, moose, lynx, wolverines, and numerous bird species. If you're lucky, you might even spot the iconic Norwegian musk oxen in places like Dovrefjell-Sunndalsfjella National Park.

It's worth noting that Norway has a "right to roam" policy called "allemannsretten," which grants everyone access to most uncultivated land, including national parks, for recreational activities. However, it's essential to respect nature, follow the guidelines, and leave no trace when camping or exploring these areas.

When planning a camping trip to Norway's national parks, it's advisable to research and prepare adequately. Check the weather conditions, pack appropriate gear, and make sure you have sufficient supplies, including food and water. Additionally, always prioritize safety and be mindful of the potential challenges posed by Norway's diverse and sometimes unpredictable nature.

In summary, camping in Norway's national parks offers a remarkable opportunity to connect with nature, immerse yourself in stunning landscapes, and engage in various outdoor activities. From hiking majestic mountains to fishing in pristine lakes and observing captivating wildlife, Norway's national parks provide a truly unforgettable camping experience.

Chapter 8. Norwegian Cuisine and Local Delicacies

Traditional Norwegian Dishes

Norway, known for its stunning landscapes and rich cultural heritage, also boasts a diverse and delicious culinary tradition. Traditional Norwegian dishes are often influenced by the country's geography, climate, and history. Here are some popular Norwegian dishes that have been enjoyed for generations:

1. Lutefisk: Lutefisk is a unique dish made from dried whitefish, typically cod, that has been soaked in water and lye for several days, then rehydrated and cooked. It has a gelatinous texture and is often served with boiled potatoes, peas, bacon, and a creamy white sauce.

2. Rakfisk: Rakfisk is a traditional Norwegian dish made from fermented freshwater fish, typically trout or char. The fish is salted and left to ferment for a few months before being served. Rakfisk is typically enjoyed on flatbread with sour cream, onions, and potatoes.

3. Pinnekjøtt: Pinnekjøtt is a favourite dish during the Christmas season in Norway. It consists of lamb

ribs that have been salted and dried, then steamed over birch branches. The result is tender, flavorful meat that is traditionally served with mashed rutabaga and boiled potatoes.

4. Fårikål: Fårikål is often considered Norway's national dish. It is a simple and hearty stew made from lamb, cabbage, whole black peppercorns, and water. The ingredients are layered in a pot and cooked slowly until the meat is tender and the flavours have melded together.

5. Raspeballer/Klubb: Raspeballer, also known as klubb, are traditional Norwegian potato dumplings. Grated raw potatoes are mixed with cooked, mashed potatoes, flour, and salt, and formed into balls. They are boiled until cooked and served with bacon, sausages, and melted butter.

6. Raspeballer med saltkjøtt og kålrabistappe: This is a variation of the previous dish where the potato dumplings are served with boiled salted meat (saltkjøtt) and mashed rutabaga (kålrabistappe). It is a popular dish in the western parts of Norway.

7. Rømmegrøt: Rømmegrøt is a traditional sour cream porridge made from sour cream, flour, and butter. It is cooked until thick and creamy and

served with melted butter, sugar, and cinnamon on top. Rømmegrøt is often enjoyed during festive occasions or as a dessert.

8. Smalahove: Smalahove is a traditional dish from Western Norway that might be considered more adventurous by some. It is made from the head of a sheep that has been salted, dried, and then smoked. The head is traditionally served whole, and the tender meat from the cheeks and tongue is enjoyed.

These are just a few examples of the many traditional Norwegian dishes you can find in Norway. The country's cuisine embraces the use of local ingredients and reflects the heritage and traditions of its people. When visiting Norway, trying these traditional dishes is a great way to immerse yourself in the country's culture and culinary delights.

Seafood and Fish Specialties

Norway, a country renowned for its breathtaking fjords and abundant marine resources, offers a wide variety of seafood and fish specialties. With a long coastline and numerous lakes and rivers, Norway has developed a deep-rooted fishing and aquaculture industry that produces some of the world's finest seafood. Let's explore some of the popular seafood and fish specialties found in Norway.

1. Salmon: Norwegian salmon is celebrated globally for its exceptional quality and taste. The country is one of the largest exporters of salmon, and its fjords provide the perfect environment for farming this prized fish. Whether enjoyed smoked, grilled, baked, or raw in dishes like sushi and sashimi, Norwegian salmon is renowned for its firm flesh, delicate flavour, and vibrant pink colour.

2. Cod: Cod is a staple in Norwegian cuisine and holds significant cultural and historical importance. Traditional Norwegian dishes like bacalao (salted cod stew), klippfisk (dried and salted cod), and lutefisk (dried cod treated with lye) showcase the versatility of this whitefish. Cod is appreciated for its mild flavor, flaky texture, and ability to be prepared in numerous ways.

3. Arctic Char: Arctic char, a cold-water fish closely related to salmon and trout, thrives in the clean and pristine waters of Norway. Known for its delicate flavour and distinctive reddish-pink flesh, it is often served grilled, baked, or pan-seared. The rich taste and high fat content make it a popular choice for seafood enthusiasts.

4. King Crab: Norway is home to the mighty king crab, an impressive crustacean that has become a sought-after delicacy worldwide. The cold waters of the Barents Sea provide the perfect habitat for these giant crabs. Known for their large size and succulent meat, king crabs are typically served steamed or boiled with melted butter or incorporated into various seafood dishes.

5. Shrimp: Norwegian cold-water shrimp, often called "North Atlantic shrimp" or "nordhavsräkor," are small, sweet, and flavorful. These pink delicacies are usually boiled and peeled, making them a popular addition to salads, sandwiches, or served with aioli as a starter or snack.

6. Mackerel: Mackerel is a common fish found along the Norwegian coast and is enjoyed for its distinctively rich and oily flesh. Often grilled, smoked, or pickled, mackerel is appreciated for its strong flavour and high omega-3 fatty acid content.

7. Herring: Herring has been a vital part of Norwegian cuisine for centuries. Pickled or marinated herring is a common delicacy, often served with sour cream, onions, and potatoes. Herring is also used in traditional dishes like

rollmops (herring fillets rolled with pickles) and lutefisk.

These are just a few examples of the seafood and fish specialties that Norway has to offer. The country's commitment to sustainable fishing practices ensures the availability of high-quality seafood while preserving marine ecosystems. Whether you're a seafood lover or an adventurous foodie, Norway's diverse range of seafood and fish dishes will undoubtedly leave you craving for more.

Scandinavian Desserts and Pastries

Norway, located in Scandinavia, has a rich culinary tradition that includes a variety of delicious desserts and pastries. Scandinavian desserts and pastries in Norway often incorporate local ingredients such as berries, oats, and dairy products, resulting in unique and flavorful treats. Here are some notable Scandinavian desserts and pastries you can find in Norway:

1. Krumkake: Krumkake is a delicate and crispy wafer-like cookie that is often rolled into a cone shape. It is made from a batter of flour, sugar, butter, and cream, which is cooked on a special iron griddle. Krumkake is typically enjoyed during

festive occasions and is often filled with whipped cream or jams.

2. Kladdkaka: Although kladdkaka originated in Sweden, it has gained popularity in Norway as well. Kladdkaka is a dense and gooey chocolate cake with a slightly undercooked centre. It is typically served with a dusting of powdered sugar and a dollop of whipped cream.

3. Bløtkake: Bløtkake, also known as Norwegian cream cake, is a classic celebration cake in Norway. It consists of layers of sponge cake, whipped cream, and fresh berries or fruit. Bløtkake is often decorated with marzipan, chocolate shavings, and additional fruits.

4. Skillingsboller: Skillingsboller, also known as cinnamon rolls, are a staple in Scandinavian baking. These sweet and aromatic pastries are made from a yeast dough infused with cinnamon and cardamom. Skillingsboller are typically baked until golden brown and topped with pearl sugar.

5. Fyrstekake: Fyrstekake, or Prince's Cake, is a traditional Norwegian almond tart. The crust is made from a buttery dough that is pressed into a tart pan. The filling is a rich almond paste flavored

with cardamom. Fyrstekake is often decorated with a lattice pattern on top and dusted with powdered sugar.

6. Multekrem: Multekrem is a simple yet delicious Norwegian dessert made with cloudberries and whipped cream. Cloudberries are wild berries that grow in the Norwegian mountains and have a unique tart and sweet flavor. The berries are usually served with whipped cream and sometimes a sprinkle of sugar.

7. Pepperkaker: Pepperkaker are traditional Norwegian gingerbread cookies often associated with the Christmas season. They are made from a spiced dough flavoured with ginger, cinnamon, cloves, and black pepper. Pepperkaker are usually cut into various shapes, such as hearts, stars, and animals, and can be decorated with icing.

These are just a few examples of the delightful Scandinavian desserts and pastries you can find in Norway. Each treat has its own distinct flavours and holds a special place in Norwegian cuisine, often enjoyed during festive occasions or as comforting treats throughout the year.

Culinary Festivals and Food Markets

Norway, known for its stunning landscapes and rich cultural heritage, also offers a delightful array of culinary festivals and food markets that showcase the country's unique cuisine and local produce. From traditional dishes to innovative creations, these events celebrate Norway's gastronomic heritage and provide a platform for both locals and visitors to explore the country's diverse food scene. Let's delve into some notable culinary festivals and food markets in Norway.

1. Gladmat Festival (Stavanger): Gladmat is one of Norway's largest food festivals, held annually in Stavanger. This vibrant event showcases an extensive range of food stalls, where visitors can sample everything from seafood delicacies to reindeer dishes and traditional Norwegian pastries. Local and international chefs demonstrate their skills, and various culinary competitions and workshops take place throughout the festival.

2. Mathallen (Oslo): Located in the vibrant Grünerløkka district of Oslo, Mathallen is a bustling food market that attracts food enthusiasts from near and far. It offers an impressive selection of local and international ingredients, artisanal products, and ready-to-eat meals. From freshly

caught seafood and cured meats to artisanal cheeses and homemade chocolates, Mathallen provides a sensory journey through Norway's culinary delights.

3. Rakfisk Festival (Fagernes): Rakfisk, a traditional Norwegian dish consisting of fermented fish, is celebrated at the Rakfisk Festival in Fagernes. This unique event brings together local producers and enthusiasts of this pungent delicacy. Visitors can taste different varieties of rakfisk, learn about the traditional production methods, and experience live music and cultural performances.

4. Bergen Fish Market (Bergen): Situated in the heart of Bergen, the historic Bergen Fish Market offers a vibrant and authentic seafood experience. Here, you can find an impressive assortment of fresh fish, shellfish, and other marine delicacies straight from the Norwegian coast. Local vendors and fishermen proudly display their catches, and visitors can savour traditional dishes like fish soup, smoked salmon, and grilled seafood.

5. Trøndersk Matfestival (Trondheim): Trøndersk Matfestival in Trondheim celebrates the culinary traditions of the Trøndelag region. This festival highlights the best local ingredients, such as

berries, game, and dairy products. Visitors can explore food stalls, taste traditional dishes, and engage with local producers. Cooking competitions, culinary workshops, and live entertainment add to the festive atmosphere.

6. Røros Matfestival (Røros): The Røros Matfestival takes place in the charming UNESCO World Heritage Site of Røros. This event showcases regional specialties, including cured meats, cheese, and traditional bread. Local farmers, producers, and chefs gather to promote sustainable food practices and highlight the unique flavours of the area. The festival also features food-related seminars, exhibitions, and cultural performances.

These culinary festivals and food markets in Norway offer a fantastic opportunity to discover and indulge in the country's diverse culinary traditions. Whether you're a food lover, a curious traveller, or someone seeking a taste of Norway's rich heritage, these events provide a memorable experience filled with delicious flavours, warm hospitality, and cultural immersion.

Recommended Restaurants and Cafes

Norway offers a diverse culinary scene with a wide range of restaurants and cafes that cater to various tastes and preferences. From traditional Norwegian cuisine to international flavours, here are some recommended restaurants and cafes in Norway:

1. Maaemo (Oslo): Maaemo is a three-Michelin-starred restaurant in Oslo, known for its innovative and artistic approach to Norwegian cuisine. It focuses on locally sourced and seasonal ingredients, creating unique and memorable dining experiences.

2. Fru Hagen (Oslo): Fru Hagen is a cozy and popular cafe located in the Grünerløkka neighbourhood of Oslo. It offers a relaxed atmosphere, delicious brunch options, sandwiches, cakes, and a wide range of beverages, including craft beers and cocktails.

3. Lysverket (Bergen): Situated in Bergen's KODE Art Museum, Lysverket combines art, culture, and gastronomy. This modern and stylish restaurant offers a menu inspired by local produce and Nordic flavours, with a focus on sustainability and contemporary cuisine.

4. Baklandet Skydsstation (Trondheim): Housed in a historic building in Trondheim, Baklandet Skydsstation is a charming cafe known for its

traditional Norwegian fare. It serves dishes like reindeer stew, fish cakes, and hearty sandwiches, accompanied by homemade pastries and coffee.

5. Cornelius Seafood Restaurant (Bergen): Located on a small island near Bergen, Cornelius Seafood Restaurant offers a unique dining experience with stunning views of the fjords. It specialises in seafood delicacies, serving freshly caught fish, shellfish, and other maritime delights.

6. Renaa Matbaren (Stavanger): Renaa Matbaren in Stavanger is a trendy and vibrant restaurant that focuses on locally sourced ingredients. It offers a menu inspired by both traditional and modern Norwegian cuisine, with dishes like cured salmon, lamb, and Nordic-inspired desserts.

7. Mathallen (Oslo): Mathallen is a vibrant food hall in Oslo, showcasing a variety of culinary delights. It features numerous food stalls, restaurants, and shops where you can explore and taste a wide range of local and international cuisines, from seafood to gourmet burgers and artisanal chocolates.

8. Solvold's Cafeteria (Ålesund): Solvolds Cafeteria is a classic Norwegian cafeteria located in Ålesund. It has been serving traditional Norwegian dishes for

over a century. You can enjoy dishes like fish soup, open-faced sandwiches, and homemade cakes while taking in the beautiful views of the harbour.

9. Nama Sushi (Tromsø): Nama Sushi in Tromsø is a popular spot for sushi lovers. It offers a wide selection of fresh and creative sushi rolls, sashimi, and other Japanese specialties, all prepared with high-quality ingredients.

10. Huset (Longyearbyen, Svalbard): Huset is a unique restaurant located in the Arctic town of Longyearbyen on the Svalbard archipelago. It combines a cosy atmosphere with a diverse menu featuring reindeer, seal, and other local Arctic ingredients, as well as international dishes.

These are just a few examples of the many fantastic restaurants and cafes you can find throughout Norway. Whether you're seeking traditional Norwegian flavours or exploring international cuisines, Norway has something to offer for every palate.

Chapter 9. Practical Information and Travel Tips

Accommodation Options

When planning a trip to Norway, it's essential to consider your accommodation options to ensure a comfortable and enjoyable stay. Norway offers a wide range of accommodation choices, catering to various budgets, preferences, and travel styles. Whether you're looking for luxury hotels, cozy guesthouses, or unique stays, Norway has something for everyone. Here are some popular accommodation options to consider when visiting this beautiful Scandinavian country:

1. Hotels: Norway boasts a range of hotels, from internationally renowned luxury chains to charming boutique accommodations. Major cities like Oslo, Bergen, and Trondheim offer a plethora of hotel choices with varying price ranges. Many hotels in Norway feature modern amenities, stunning views, and convenient locations, making them ideal for travellers seeking comfort and convenience.

2. Guesthouses and Bed & Breakfasts: For a more personal touch and a chance to interact with local hosts, guesthouses and bed & breakfasts are

excellent options. These cosy establishments often offer comfortable rooms, hearty breakfasts, and a homely atmosphere. They can be found in both urban and rural areas, providing a unique glimpse into Norwegian culture and hospitality.

3. Cabins and Holiday Homes: Norway's picturesque landscapes make it an ideal destination for renting cabins or holiday homes. From charming wooden cottages in the countryside to modern waterfront villas along the fjords, these accommodations offer a rustic and private experience. Many cabins come equipped with kitchens, saunas, and fireplaces, allowing visitors to enjoy the country's natural beauty while enjoying the comforts of home.

4. Hostels: Budget-conscious travellers and backpackers will find an array of hostels across Norway. Hostels are an excellent option for those looking to meet fellow travellers and explore Norway on a tighter budget. They offer dormitory-style accommodations with shared facilities like kitchens and common areas. Some hostels even provide private rooms for those seeking more privacy.

5. Farm Stays: Embracing Norway's rural charm, farm stays provide visitors with an immersive experience in the country's agricultural landscapes. Guests can stay in traditional farmhouses, participate in daily farm activities, and enjoy fresh, locally sourced meals. Farm stays are particularly popular in the rural regions of Telemark, Valdres, and Trøndelag.

6. Unique Stays: Norway offers some truly unique accommodation options that will make your trip even more memorable. From staying in a historic lighthouse or a converted fisherman's cottage to sleeping in an ice hotel or a treehouse, these unconventional choices allow travellers to experience Norway in a distinctive way.

When booking accommodation in Norway, it's advisable to plan in advance, especially during peak travel seasons. Additionally, consider the location of your chosen accommodation as Norway's natural attractions are spread across the country. Whether you prefer urban comforts or a serene countryside retreat, Norway's accommodation options ensure a delightful stay, making your visit to this Scandinavian gem even more remarkable.

Health and Safety

Norway, known for its breathtaking natural landscapes and vibrant cities, also places great importance on health and safety. Whether you're exploring the picturesque fjords, hiking in the majestic mountains, or strolling through the charming streets of Oslo, it's crucial to prioritise your well-being. Here's some valuable information to keep in mind regarding health and safety in Norway.

1. Healthcare System:
Norway boasts a highly efficient and well-regarded healthcare system. Both residents and tourists have access to excellent medical care. Hospitals and clinics are equipped with modern facilities, and healthcare professionals are highly trained. In case of a medical emergency, dial 113 for immediate assistance.

2. Travel Insurance:
Before visiting Norway, it is strongly recommended to have comprehensive travel insurance that covers medical expenses, trip cancellations, and personal liability. Ensure that your insurance policy provides sufficient coverage for outdoor activities like hiking and skiing, which are popular in Norway.

3. Vaccinations:
No specific vaccinations are required to enter Norway. However, it is advisable to ensure that routine vaccinations are up to date. It's best to consult your healthcare provider or refer to the official website of your country's health department for the most accurate and current information.

4. Water Quality:
Tap water in Norway is of excellent quality and is safe to drink across the country. You can refill your water bottle from taps or fountains without any concerns. This not only helps reduce plastic waste but also keeps you hydrated during your explorations.

5. Food Safety:
Norway maintains high standards of food safety. Restaurants, cafes, and eateries adhere to strict hygiene regulations. While dining out, it is generally safe to enjoy Norwegian cuisine. However, remember to follow basic food safety practices such as washing your hands before eating and opting for reputable establishments.

6. Outdoor Safety:
Norway's breathtaking landscapes offer endless opportunities for outdoor activities. However, it's

important to be mindful of potential risks. Before embarking on hikes or outdoor adventures, check weather conditions, follow marked trails, and inform others about your plans. It's also wise to carry essential safety equipment, such as sturdy footwear, appropriate clothing, maps, and a charged phone.

7. Sun Protection:
Even in Norway's northern regions, the sun can be intense during the summer months. Protect your skin by wearing sunscreen, sunglasses, and a hat. Remember to stay hydrated, especially if engaging in outdoor activities for an extended period.

8. Emergency Services:
In case of emergencies, dial 112 to reach the police, fire department, or ambulance services. Norway's emergency response system is reliable and ensures prompt assistance when needed.

By staying aware and taking necessary precautions, you can have a safe and enjoyable journey throughout Norway. Remember to respect the environment, follow local regulations, and take care of yourself and others as you explore this stunning Scandinavian country.

Etiquette and Customs

Norway, a country renowned for its breathtaking natural landscapes, rich cultural heritage, and warm hospitality, also has its unique set of customs and etiquette. Understanding and respecting these customs will help you make the most of your travel experience and ensure positive interactions with locals. Here are some key points to keep in mind when visiting Norway:

1. Punctuality: Norwegians value punctuality and appreciate it when others arrive on time. Whether it's meeting friends, attending appointments, or catching public transportation, it's considered polite to be prompt.

2. Personal Space: Norwegians generally have a larger personal space compared to some other cultures. It's advisable to maintain a comfortable distance and avoid unnecessary physical contact unless you are well-acquainted with someone.

3. Tipping: Tipping is not obligatory in Norway, as a service charge is often included in the bill. However, if you receive excellent service, it is appreciated to leave a small tip as a gesture of appreciation.

4. Greeting Customs: When meeting someone for the first time or entering a shop, it is customary to greet with a firm handshake and direct eye contact. Norwegians appreciate polite and friendly greetings.

5. Dress Code: Norwegians generally dress modestly and casually. In urban areas, smart casual attire is suitable for most occasions, while outdoor activities may require more practical clothing due to the climate and terrain.

6. Queuing: Norwegians have a strong respect for queues and lines. It's essential to wait patiently for your turn and avoid cutting in front of others. This etiquette applies in various situations, such as public transportation, shops, or attractions.

7. Nature and Environment: Norway's natural beauty is a cherished asset, and Norwegians take great pride in preserving it. When exploring outdoor areas, it is crucial to respect nature, follow marked trails, and dispose of waste responsibly. Leave no trace and take care to keep the surroundings clean.

8. Silence and Privacy: Norwegians often value personal privacy and appreciate moments of

silence. When using public transportation or visiting quiet spaces, such as libraries or museums, it is polite to maintain a quiet demeanor.

9. Alcohol Consumption: Norway has strict regulations regarding alcohol sales and consumption. The legal drinking age is 18 for milder alcoholic beverages and 20 for stronger ones. It is not customary to drink excessively in public or to be visibly intoxicated.

10. Social Equality: Norway is known for its emphasis on social equality and egalitarianism. When interacting with Norwegians, it is important to treat everyone with respect and equality, regardless of their gender, occupation, or social status.

Remember, these customs and etiquette guidelines are general observations and may vary depending on the specific region or individual preferences. However, by demonstrating cultural sensitivity and being mindful of local customs, you will undoubtedly enhance your travel experience in Norway and forge meaningful connections with the locals.

Useful Phrases and Basic Norwegian

Here are some useful phrases and basic Norwegian expressions that can come in handy when communicating in Norway:

1. Hello/Hi - Hei (pronounced "hay")
2. Good morning - God morgen (pronounced "goh morn")
3. Good afternoon - God ettermiddag (pronounced "goh aht-ter-mee-dahg")
4. Good evening - God kveld (pronounced "goh kveld")
5. Goodbye - Ha det (pronounced "hah deh")
6. Please - Vær så snill (pronounced "vair saw snill")
7. Thank you - Takk (pronounced "tahk")
8. You're welcome - Vær så god (pronounced "vair saw goh")
9. Yes - Ja (pronounced "yah")
10. No - Nei (pronounced "nay")
11. Excuse me - Unnskyld (pronounced "oonn-skilled")
12. I'm sorry - Jeg beklager (pronounced "yay beh-kla-ger")
13. Do you speak English? - Snakker du engelsk? (pronounced "snah-kker du eng-elsk?")
14. I don't understand - Jeg forstår ikke (pronounced "yay for-stohr eenteh")

15. Could you repeat that, please? - Kan du gjenta det, vær så snill? (pronounced "kahn doo yep-tah deht, vair saw snill?")
16. Where is the restroom? - Hvor er toalettet? (pronounced "vohr air toh-let-et?")
17. How much does it cost? - Hvor mye koster det? (pronounced "vohr moo-eh koh-stehr deht?")
18. I need help - Jeg trenger hjelp (pronounced "yay tren-ger yelp")
19. What's your name? - Hva heter du? (pronounced "vah heh-ter doo?")
20. Nice to meet you - Hyggelig å møte deg (pronounced "hoog-eh-lee oh moh-teh deh")

These phrases should help you in basic conversations and interactions in Norwegian. Remember to pronounce the words clearly and politely, as Norwegians appreciate the effort to speak their language.

Packing List and Essential Gear

When visiting Norway, especially if you plan to explore its stunning natural landscapes, it's important to pack appropriately to ensure your comfort, safety, and enjoyment. Here's a packing list of essential gear and items to consider for your trip to Norway:

1. Clothing:

 - Layered clothing: Norway's weather can be unpredictable, so pack a combination of lightweight and warm layers. This allows you to adjust your clothing according to the temperature.

 - Waterproof jacket: Invest in a good quality, breathable waterproof jacket to protect yourself from rain and wind.

 - Insulated clothing: Bring a warm, insulated jacket or fleece for colder days and evenings.

 - Waterproof pants: Consider waterproof pants or hiking trousers to stay dry during outdoor activities.

 - Hiking boots: Sturdy, waterproof hiking boots with good ankle support are essential for hiking and exploring Norway's rugged terrain.

 - Woolen or thermal socks: Pack several pairs of warm, moisture-wicking socks to keep your feet comfortable during outdoor adventures.

 - Hat, gloves, and scarf: Don't forget to pack warm accessories for extra protection against the cold.

2. Outdoor Gear:

 - Backpack: A comfortable and spacious backpack is essential for day hikes or longer excursions.

 - Water bottle: Norway has an abundance of clean, drinkable water. Carry a reusable water bottle to stay hydrated while minimizing plastic waste.

- Trekking poles: If you plan on hiking challenging trails, consider bringing trekking poles for stability and support.
  - Map and compass: While modern technology provides navigation assistance, having a physical map and compass is crucial in case of battery failure or loss of signal.
  - Headlamp or flashlight: Useful for hiking in low light conditions or exploring caves and tunnels.
  - Sleeping bag: If you're camping or staying in mountain huts, a lightweight, compact sleeping bag is recommended.

3. Safety and Survival:
  - First aid kit: Carry a basic first aid kit with essential items such as band-aids, antiseptic ointment, pain relievers, and any necessary personal medications.
  - Emergency whistle: A whistle can be used to signal for help in case of an emergency.
  - Survival blanket: A lightweight and compact survival blanket provides warmth and protection in emergency situations.
  - Sunscreen and sunglasses: Even in colder months, the sun can be intense, especially in the mountains. Protect your skin and eyes accordingly.

4. Electronics and Miscellaneous:

- Power adapter: Norway uses Type C and F plugs, so make sure to bring a suitable adapter for charging your electronic devices.

- Portable charger: Keep your devices powered up, especially if you're relying on your smartphone for navigation.

- Camera: Norway's breathtaking landscapes are perfect for photography enthusiasts, so consider bringing a camera to capture those memorable moments.

- Cash and cards: Although Norway is largely a cashless society, it's still useful to carry some cash for small purchases or emergencies.

Remember to pack according to the season and specific activities you plan to undertake. It's also a good idea to check the weather forecast for your travel dates and consult local resources for any additional gear recommendations.